African Religions: A Very Short Introduction

VERY SHORT INTRODUCTIONS are for anyone wanting a stimulating and accessible way into a new subject. They are written by experts, and have been translated into more than 45 different languages.

The series began in 1995, and now covers a wide variety of topics in every discipline. The VSI library now contains over 500 volumes—a Very Short Introduction to everything from Psychology and Philosophy of Science to American History and Relativity—and continues to grow in every subject area.

Titles in the series include the following:

Jacob K. Olupona

AFRICAN RELIGIONS

A Very Short Introduction

OXFORD
UNIVERSITY PRESS

OXFORD
UNIVERSITY PRESS

Oxford University Press is a department of the University of Oxford.
It furthers the University's objective of excellence in research,
scholarship, and education by publishing worldwide.

Oxford   New York

Auckland   Cape Town   Dar es Salaam   Hong Kong   Karachi
Kuala Lumpur   Madrid   Melbourne   Mexico City   Nairobi
New Delhi   Shanghai   Taipei   Toronto

With offices in

Argentina   Austria   Brazil   Chile   Czech Republic   France   Greece
Guatemala   Hungary   Italy   Japan   Poland   Portugal   Singapore
South Korea   Switzerland   Thailand   Turkey   Ukraine   Vietnam

Oxford is a registered trade mark of Oxford University Press
in the UK and certain other countries.

Published in the United States of America by
Oxford University Press
198 Madison Avenue, New York, NY 10016

Library of Congress Cataloging-in-Publication Data
is available.
ISBN: 978-0-19-979058-6

12

Printed in Great Britain
by Ashford Colour Press Ltd., Gosport, Hants.
on acid-free paper

This book is dedicated to my students past and present, in appreciation for their ideas, diligence, inspiration, and encouragement, in giving me hope during my moments of despair about the state of scholarship on Africa.

Contents

List of illustrations

Acknowledgments

It has been quite an interesting exercise working on this short introduction to African religions. Let me thank my research assistants who have helped with researching some of the materials for this book: Lisanne Norman, Kyrah Daniels, Venise Battle, Adam McGee, Ayodeji Ogunnaike, and Sheila Winborne. To the museums and my colleagues who allowed me to use in this book photographs from their collections, I say a big thank-you.

Preface

In order to provide a fuller picture of African religions, there must be more productive distinctions between the study of African religion as object and the study of African religion as subject. The vast majority of writings about African religions has treated Africa as Other, highlighting its differences from Western culture and, in many cases, casting these differences as deficiencies. Many of the West's greatest thinkers and artists have, unfortunately, used Africa as a screen onto which they could project their worst nightmares and racist anxieties. Hegel perceived Africa as a land of primitivism, which had nothing to contribute to civilization. Joseph Conrad used the African continent as a metaphor for the blackest reaches of the human soul. President Nicolas Sarkozy of France, in a speech to the University of Dakar students, similarly disparaged African myth-history by claiming that Africans' continual adherence to its mythic past is responsible for its underdevelopment and its cycle of poverty. "The tragedy of Africa is that the African has not fully entered into history. . . . They have never really launched themselves into the future," Sarkozy claimed. He continued the insult, stating, "The African peasant only knew the eternal renewal of time, marked by the endless repetition of the same gestures and the same words." These comments, unfortunately, resemble the late Mircea Eliade's description of indigenous spirituality. Sarkozy was totally oblivious to how the West's interference in African affairs in a neocolonial situation fifty years after independence has continued to undermine the continent's social and economic growth and prosperity.

Meanwhile, Africa has long had its own scholarly tradition. Beginning in its ancient past during the precolonial period when native artists and custodians and interpreters of Africa's oral traditions—such as diviners, griots, and the like—became the envy of early European explorers who marveled at their creativity and intellectual acumen. During the fourteenth century, formal West African scholarship in the sciences, arts, and medicine began, as Islamic universities were instituted in the medieval empires of Mali, Songhai, and Kanem-Bornu. In the fifteenth century, Catholic missionaries arrived in Warri, Kongo, and the Benin Kingdom, while European adventurers, most lacking scholarly training, visited Africa and returned to Europe to record their findings in what amounted to the first known studies of indigenous African religious traditions. Their research contributed directly to Europe's plunder of Africa, by providing evidence of the supposed inferiority of African culture and of Africans' need for Europeans to lead them forcefully toward "civilization." This ideology was captured succinctly in Belgium's motto for its murderous reign in the Congo, *"dominer pour servir"* (dominate in order to serve). Many early European scholars viewed African indigenous religions as primitive compared with Christianity, and promoted the idea of an African mind and thought system inferior to the European. Africans were pronounced incapable of producing meaningful, sophisticated religious traditions and were said to lack "true knowledge" of a Supreme God. If anything showed a level of sophistication that would seem contrary to such beliefs, then it was proposed that African civilizations and religious belief systems must have originated elsewhere and been transported to the African continent. Such views, called "diffusionist," held that cultures in west and west-central Africa had gradually "trickled down" into the continent—in degraded form, naturally—from the great Mediterranean centers of civilization. Thus, early scholarship on Africa and African religions reflected a pernicious racism, which rendered impossible the kinds of sensitivity to human spirituality that would lead to a genuine appreciation of Africa's profound and inspiring religious culture.

Some of the most serious early writings about African religions were produced by European missionaries sent to Africa to spread Christianity. For these missionaries, the study of African religion was ultimately a *preparatio evangelia*, a necessary step toward understanding the most expedient way to convert Africans to Christianity. Such missionary activities were rarely disinterested but tended also to accompany efforts to establish trade and colonialism. In short, Christians were seen as likely to make better business partners and workers. Nonetheless, while we may find the motivation to be unsavory in the extreme, the point remains that some of these missionary reports provided valuable historical insights into African religions and African life more broadly.

In the 1960s, African universities encouraged a revitalized study of African religions, reflecting Africa's new nation-state status and emergent spirit of freedom and pride. In Nigeria, Uganda, Kenya, Ghana, and elsewhere, African institutions of higher learning acknowledged their religious pluralism and encouraged the study of Islam and African traditional religions alongside Christianity. Inspired by political independence, a religiously pluralistic national identity emerged in many regions, anchored in a belief in a Supreme God, which each of the three dominant religions shared. This religious vitality also helped the African people to resist oppression.

Gradually, the study of African religions developed as an autonomous field within the comparative history of religion. However, many of the significant figures who helped develop the field were trained in Christian religious studies, many in theology. Such scholars included John Mbiti, Geoffrey Parrinder, Bọ́lájí

Ìdòwú, and Father Placide Tempels. In many cases, these scholars, who had been trained in more conventional religious studies, came to study and teach African traditional religions when they recognized that it was vital for someone to do so. However, their training predisposed them to see African traditional religions through the lens of Christian theology, for which reason their work has often been criticized by subsequent generations of secular scholars. In spite of this, their works often remain quite relevant and indeed have remained durable classics in the field.

During the 1980s and 1990s, Africans began to study abroad in significant and increasing numbers. African scholars who chose to pursue the study of religion outside of seminaries often landed in the fields of phenomenology and the comparative history of religions. These disciplines addressed the grand questions of the history, meanings, and functions of belief systems in a comparative fashion. In addition, they tended to focus on the relationship between centers and peripheries of religious traditions. Until recently, preoccupation with "centers" (i.e., Rome for Catholics, Khalistan for Sikhs, Mecca for Muslims, and Ilé-Ifè for Yorùbá) created disengagement with diaspora formations of religious practices as subjects of study. Upon returning to their homeland universities, young scholars injected into religious studies curricula a degree of scientific objectivity, which was often at odds with the pervasive theological and ecumenical trends in their home countries. Paradoxically, this period, coinciding with the decline of African economies, witnessed innovative scholarship in African religions.

This period also saw the rise of numerous British and American trained scholars of African and African diaspora religions who, in many ways, have shaped the course of the discipline during the last thirty years. The work of these scholars is characterized by both a commitment to working across disciplines and a view of Africa and the African diaspora as parts of the larger black Atlantic, which must be viewed as a unity in order to arrive at a nuanced interpretation of its religious history. Some scholars of African religions are now examining how religion is implicated in the human and social crises dominating discourse on Africa—poverty, environmental degradation, HIV/AIDS, disease, corruption, ethnic and religious violence, and civil war. Since religion, alongside ethnic strife, is identified as a source of violent conflict throughout the continent, these scholars are equally engaged in various policy considerations concerned with ameliorating the crises confronting the continent. The "neutral," socially disengaged scholar who once dominated the study of African religion is increasingly seen as ineffectual in discussing a continent in crisis. African scholars today feel morally obligated to address religion as it relates to immediate and pressing human concerns, and as such, they serve as models for the entire academy.

A new generation of scholars of the African and African diaspora religion is breaking radically from the earlier trends. Those studying black Atlantic formations are focusing on the prevalence and transformation of African religious practices and cosmologies in the Americas, and exploring the social histories and cultural practices of African captives transported to the Americas. Others interested in the spread of Christianity and Islamic religious practices among diaspora Africans are engaged in tracing the spread of these traditions and conversion in the United States, Europe, and elsewhere. With the goal of understanding the adaptation of African practices in the Americas, studies of African religions in the black Atlantic have focused on religious communities in the African diaspora—communities of survivors and their descendants who confronted racial segregation alongside gender and sexual discrimination. Incorporating race, ethnicity, gender, and sexuality as units of analysis, interdisciplinary approaches greatly enhance the study of diaspora religion. These emerging scholars are concerned with destabilizing the traditional centers and peripheries of religious studies, and are instead focusing on religious adaptation and invention. As markers of black Atlantic cultural life, African-derived religions continue to be essential to understanding the lives of people outside the African continent.

Perhaps one of the most exciting revolutions taking place in African and African diaspora religious studies is the rapid increase in the number of scholar-practitioners. The vast majority of scholars who have studied African traditional religions and African diaspora religions have been adherents to other religions or have been areligious. While the anthropological emphasis on participant observation has generated many insights into the lived religious experiences of practitioners, scholar-practitioners argue that many of the nuances of African and African diaspora religions remain closed to those who are not themselves devotees. Scholars like Asare Opoku and Wande Abimbola, a traditional babaláwo (Ifá diviner), have dramatically shifted the questions that occupy the field by insisting that all scholars in the field take seriously the concerns and interests of practitioners.

What, then, will prove critical in the study of African and African diaspora religious studies in the next few decades? A new paradigm is needed that views African religious experience and expression through a more comprehensive and holistic prism. This book is an attempt to do just that by looking at African religions through a broad variety of disciplinary lenses. Its goal is to provide a fuller picture of what these traditions are and do for their practitioners in order to inspire intellectual curiosity in readers who are encountering these traditions for the first time, while also encouraging scholars and educators to think creatively about how best to introduce these traditions to their students.

Chapter 1
Worldview, cosmology, and myths of origin

African religions are as diverse as the African continent itself. Africa is home to more than fifty countries, nearly every form of ecological niche found on Earth, and hundreds of ethnic groups who together speak more than a thousand languages. It is not surprising, then, that this enormous range of peoples, cultures, and modes of living would also be reflected in a diverse range of religious expressions. Religious worldviews, often unique to distinct ethnic groups, reflect people's identities and lie at the heart of how they relate to one another, to other people, and to the world at large. These religious worldviews encode, as well as influence, ethical practices, taboos, and the knowledge particular to each group.

Worldviews

The integration of religion into all aspects of daily life poses a sharp contrast to the church-state dichotomy upheld in Euro-American societies; African religious worldviews permeate economics and politics on the continent, where the sacred and secular realms influence one another. In fact, the use of the term "religion" is problematic when speaking of African traditional religions if one approaches the topic without questioning assumptions about what religion is, means, and does. The separation between religion and government, championed in one form or another in nearly all Western democracies, is predicated upon a particular vision of religion as something that can be extracted from public life and quarantined in its own sphere.

While the separation of church and state has, in many cases, proven more theoretical than actual, the fact that it is even believed to be possible—or desirable—reveals important Western assumptions about the nature of religion, especially as it pertains to communal life. For adherents of African traditional religions, such a separation is neither desirable nor possible, because religious beliefs inform every aspect of life—including birthing and death, marriage, family dynamics, diet, dress and grooming, health care (including mental health), the spending and saving of money, interactions with one's friends and neighbors, and of course, governance. In many traditional African governments, civic authorities were—and in some cases still are—not only arbiters of divinely appointed laws and religious leaders but are also believed to be semidivine. It would be a mistake, however, to view this suffusion of daily life with religion as evidence of religious theocracy or fundamentalism. On the contrary, it is quite normal and balanced when one begins with the assumption that religion is not a separate mode unto itself but is instead a varied and diverse set of components touching upon every aspect of life.

Indeed, religion in Africa remains the pulse of the private and public spheres, placing a strong emphasis on moral and social order in families, clans, lineages, and intraethnic interactions. As such, it pervades the daily affairs and conduct of African societies. Most traditional African societies employ two classes of morals: those pertaining to individual conduct, and those governing social and community relations. Community morals also dictate codes of conduct at the family level. These complex mandates aim to maintain balance among maternal and paternal relatives, clans, and lineages.

Religious Africans, like religious people everywhere, often ascribe supernatural origin to codes of conduct, believing that they derive from spirits, gods, and ancestors. Usually, communities maintain these edicts through the observance of taboos and ritual practices guided by priests, kings, and chiefs. African traditional religions typically strive for a this-worldly salvation—measured in terms of health, wealth, and offspring—while at the same time maintaining close contact with the otherworldly realm of the ancestors, spirits, and gods who are seen as having strong influence on the events and people in the here and now. Human and agricultural prosperity, longevity, vitality, and fertility are the central objectives of the spiritual life. Yet life's adversities also inform African conceptions of the universe.

The tribulations impeding one's successes may stem from negative spirits or malevolent practices such as witchcraft. Or they may be the result of neglect of one's mandatory secular or religious obligations to the deceased ancestory, the elderly, or to family shrines. Among the Ndembu of Zambia, a Bantu people from southern Africa, illness is seen primarily not as something that resides within the body of the patient but rather is a communal condition caused by imbalances in relationships with spirits, kinfolk, and members of one's community. In order to heal the person's body, what must actually be addressed by the healer is the underlying social and spiritual disruptions. Although Victor Turner specifically studied the Ndembu, subsequent generations of scholars have shown that Turner's findings have resonances in many traditional African societies and indeed in modern life in which, as has been medically proven, stress can lead to certain forms of illness.

Such practices warrant the prominent role of medicine men and women who are qualified to navigate the delicate moral and social balance between the good and evil forces exerted on the human realm. Similarly, diviners and priests use dreams and various divinatory techniques to ascertain revelations pertinent to the community. That traditional African religious worldviews continue to shape events in contemporary Africa is not in dispute.

The suffusion of daily life with religion happens in numerous ways. Leading up to the 2010 FIFA World Cup tournament in South Africa, there were popular assertions that the South African *sangomas*, the traditional healers and diviners, would magically impact the outcome of the games. By employing their supernatural aid, some believed they could influence the game in favor of their national team. Similarly, in a traditional wrestling contest that has metamorphosized into a spectacular professonal sport in modern Senegal called *laamb*, participants deploy magical and religious substances provided by their spiritual leaders called *marabouts* to insure their victory in the wrestling match. In a case of higher stakes, a no-nonsense traditional ruler, Ọba Akenzua, in Benin, Nigeria, ordered his chiefs and priests to perform a ritual against incessant kidnapping in the city. Sensing that the problem would not dissipate and would continue to evade the state security forces, he requested that the ritual be performed as a prophylaxis against kidnapping.

Although it is difficult to generalize about African traditional worldviews, a common denominator among them is a three-tiered model in which the human world exists sandwiched between the sky and the earth (including the underworld)—a schema that is not unique to Africa but found in many of the world's religious systems. A porous border exists between the human realm and the sky, which belongs to the gods. Similarly, although ancestors dwell inside of the earth, their activities also interject into human space. African cosmologies portray the universe as fluid, active, and impressionable, with agents from each realm constantly interacting with one another. This integrated worldview leads many practitioners of African religions to speak about the visible in tandem with the invisible. Each living and inanimate object is potentially sacred on some level. Many practitioners, for instance, revere animals for the wisdom they hold or for their potency

4

as sacrificial offerings. Similarly, certain herbs are sacred, and pharmacological teachings remain embedded in priests' and diviners' knowledge.

Cosmology and myths

The flexibility characterizing African religious traditions stems, in part, from the reliance on oral as opposed to written narratives, whose purported timelessness grants them authority. African traditional religions are communally maintained and routinely change in response to people's lived experiences and needs. The emphasis is on the core beliefs—ancestors, deities, divination, and sacrèd myths—rather than uniform doctrinal teachings. Sacred myths, especially those pertaining to the creation of the universe (cosmogonic) or to nature and the structure of the world (cosmological), describe significant events and noteworthy actors central to a particular people's worldview. These sacred stories are not static but rather undergo reinterpretation as one generation passes down the oral narratives to the next generation.

History and myths are each seen as containing truth. In many African communities, myths and history are effectively indistinguishable; both belong to the same genre. Among the Yorùbá of Nigeria, the word *ìtàn*, from the verb *tàn* (to spread), is used for legends, myths, history, and folktales. This suggests that stories are narratives that spread, pointing to their oral transmission. *Tàn* also references "to light," as in lighting a candle, thereby connoting enlightened meanings within the narratives.

Significantly, creation myths sometimes overlap with myths about a culture or social institution's origins. A myth among the people of Northern Yatenga in Burkina Faso demonstrates this. Two groups comprise the Yatenga people: the Foulse and the Nioniosse. According to this myth, the Foulse descended from the sky and the Nioniosse emerged from the earth. For this reason, ruling personnel, chiefs, and kings often arise from the first group

5

while leaders in rites relating to the earth's fertility originate from the latter. The complementarity between earth and sky parallels the equally necessary functions both groups perform in Yatenga society. Many Western religious traditions, when pressed, would identify the sky as the home of divinity and the space under the earth as unpleasant, bad, or outright evil. By contrast, many African cosmologies posit that the sky and the earth are both divine abodes in which creation and divine action take place.

What is the definition of "myth" itself? As a comparative term, it is not typically one used by people to describe their own beliefs and stories. For our purposes, "myth" refers to narratives that are regarded by a people as sacred, describe a portion of the worldview of that people, and provide significant insight into the people's rationale for their customs, traditions, beliefs, and practices. There are varieties of myths in African societies that display the diverse motifs, meanings, and functions of African oral traditions. There are stories about the origin of various African peoples; myths about how rituals came into practice; myths of migration; and stories about human mortality and the origins of death. More specifically, there are different varieties of cosmogonic myths and how they define the created world, people, the physical environment, and social and cultural institutions. Primordial myths continue to hold sway on contemporary societies that regard them as sources of knowledge and as the basis of their existence and moral standards.

Central to an understanding of the dynamic of myth is an awareness of the competing modes of linear and cyclical time. Linear time refers to what most readers will recognize as their default sense of time—namely, of minutes, hours, and years passing inexorably, with an unceasing movement from the past into the future. Linear time is an arrow that travels in one direction at a constant speed. By contrast, cyclical time is like a wheel, with a set amount of time and events in time that repeat indefinitely. It is like the calendar, with its finite number of names for things (Sunday to Saturday, January to December) that follow a predictable pattern from start to finish before beginning again from the top. Much has been made of the seeming emphasis on linear time in the West versus cyclical time in Africa and other places that are often caricatured as less modern. In point of fact, linear and cyclical time are found everywhere.

In Europe and America, the emphasis may be placed more heavily on linear time. Not only does it order the day but also most festivals—both secular and sacred—which are commemorations of events that happened once, at a specific time in the past. However, there are some events that still operate on cyclical time. In Christian theology, all Christians are said to be present at the moment of the Crucifixion, making the Paschal celebration not merely a reenactment or commemoration but a taking part in the original event itself that repeats every year. In the African Anglican tradition, the wedding ceremonies in cathedrals and churches begin with a popular song that references the primordial wedding in the garden of Eden, a ritual invocation of a famous song, "the Blessings said in the Garden of Eden in the first human marriage remains forever true." The song is a ritual invocation of Adam and Eve's archetypal wedding. Many traditional African festivals are kin to this, closely tied to agricultural and natural cycles.

Less focus has been given to the fact that many African festivals are of a linear sort, celebrating historical events such as the acts of kings and famous conquests. And of course, Islam has brought with it a host of celebrations tied to historical events, in particular those commemorating the lives and acts of Prophet Muhammad and his immediate deputies and successors called the Rashidun Caliphs. That is, they were perceived by Muslims as divinely chosen and guided by God to rule the community after the death of the prophet Muhammed.

Ceremonial events and ritual activities typically take place on special occasions or at times determined by a religious leader through divination or following a ritual calendar. It is particularly significant to note that many of these ceremonies and rituals depend on a cyclical notion of time, coinciding with a cosmic renewal of time. At these occasions, the cosmos is believed to have undergone a full circle and requires a reactivation or recharging in order to continue anew through a new turn of the cycle. In several African countries, the end of the year marks an important time for such renewal, a time when life is at its lowest ebb and requires rejuvenation. It is interesting that when I was growing up in a Nigerian town, the people, who were mainly converts to Christianity, referred to Christmas as *oduń kékeré* (little festival) and to the New Year as *oduń ńlá* (big festival), illustrating the significance they ascribed to the end of the year. Both notions of time and ritual cycles are embedded in African religious life and practices.

Another important aspect of the narratives that provide meaning and significance to African religious sensibility are myths. They often offer multiple renditions of the same event. Contrasting accounts regarding creation, divinities, and human agency may exist within the same ethnic group and may all be regarded as revealing some important truth. African cosmogonic narratives describe the universe's creation and attribute its formation to divine beings, but the details surrounding the universe's creation vary from story to story. In some narratives, living and nonliving beings emerge from sound. The Bambara of Mali believe that before the universe was created, there was nothing but an empty void. The cosmos began with a single sound, *Yo*, the sound at the core of creation. This sound is also a silence. Emanations from it formed the planets, stars, earth, and sentient and nonsentient beings. For the Bambara, the highest form of consciousness stems from Yo and represents itself in human beings. Unlike in several other African myths of origin in which a divine being is responsible for the act of creation, the Bambara narrative is more similar to the creation myths of Brahmanic Hinduism, in which the utterance of the primordial sound, Ohm, is seen as the first act of creation.

Another set of myths claims that the cosmos emerged from the creator's body, as detailed in a creation story from the San of southern Africa. The San believe that Tumtumbolosa, the goddess of the Gikwe people, died. Upon her death, her stomach bloated until it exploded, and the universe and its contents poured out. A river also emerged, and its fecund waters caused a forest to grow on earth. After the celestial bodies poured out, all other terrestrial beings came forth: insects, mammals, birds, reptiles, and humans. It is interesting to note the similarity between this "explosion" and the Big Bang Theory. The story, like the Genesis tales in the Jewish and Christian sacred texts, suggests that creation happened rapidly. The San and Jewish creation myths also assume a prior entity upon which creation is made. In the San story, it is the body of the goddess; in the Jewish story, it is the void. A key difference between the two is that Tumtumbolosa's death catalyzes the creative process, whereas the void is simply overwritten or pushed aside. Through death, life evolved from the decomposed body of the goddess. In both myths of origin, humankind, vegetation, and animal life emerge from the same creative process, thus establishing the kinship of ecological environments and human culture and society.

A creation-via-combustion theory also exists among the Bântu-Kôngo. The BaKongo believe the world began as an emptiness without visible life. An explosion of active forces then produced the *kalûnga*, a body of water representing vitality, force, and change. From *kalûnga* emerged other matter that combined and solidified, becoming the earth, sun, moon, and stars. From the BaKongo perspective, the earth floats in the midst of *kalûnga* and those waters separate the human world from marine life and the spirit world. Whereas other creation stories discussed in this chapter mention a specific creator or divine being responsible for generating life, Fu-Kiau reveals an African narrative of spontaneous creation. *Kalûnga* becomes a divine force, "the principle-god-of change" responsible for all of creation in motion.

Creation as emergence remains a common theme in stories from South African groups. The Xhosa cosmogonic myth says that people emerged from the underworld via a cave or deep hole. The Supreme Being enabled them to come out. The Xhosa call their place of origin *Umhlanga*, which some scholars have translated to mean "cave," but others note that among the Zulu, it means "reed" or "place of reeds." The people who remained in the place of reeds are called *abant bomlambo*, or river people. Xhosa cosmology attributes tremendous power to these beings, and they are associated with the ancestors. While most African stories focus on a creation that took place in the sky realm, the Xhosa story cites a location beneath the earth's surface, the place of the departed ancestors.

In a similar vein, the Zulu of the same region claim that the sky god Umvelinqangi married Uhlanga, a large swamp full of reeds of various colors. The sky god then used the reeds to make people in pairs of man and woman. These primordial people were called Unkulunkulu, meaning "ancestor," because each pair founded a tribe on earth. This story has corollaries in the evolutionary myth that life on earth began with aquatic beings. The story also champions the complementarity of males and females by emphasizing the generative interaction between a male sky god and a female marsh.

Often, an African creation myth identifies several lesser deities who function as a supreme being's emissaries during the creative process. The Fon of Benin Republic have a creation myth in which Nana Buluku, a creator god, births an androgynous deity named Mawu. Some versions pair Mawu with Lisa, in which case the former is female and represents the moon, while the latter is male and represents the sun. Fon mythology holds that Mawu-Lisa birthed seven sets of twins, the deities of the Voodoo pantheon. Humans, created by Mawu-Lisa's children, were placed between the sky and the underworld, to return to the Supreme Being after death.

Similarly, the Winye of Burkina Faso narrate how the creator god sent female and male twins as primordial parents to develop human life in the created world. Their offensive behavior, however, dismayed the creator; the twins utilized sorcery and resisted the natural progression of generations. The female twin withheld her offspring in her womb for a year, refusing the next generation their entrance into the world. As a result, her offspring rebelled against her and became autonomous. The original twins recognized their children's superiority and paid homage with a sacrificial goat. The Winye creation story not only accounts for the world's creation but also institutionalizes sacrifice as a corrective measure that restores social and cosmological order. It illustrates the Romanian historian of religion's argument that ritual's primary purpose is to renew time in the cosmos as well as among humans. The myth also emphasizes primordial disorder, conflict, or chaos, and the eventual reordering of the world through ritual performances. Though the disorder was, at first, a negative force, it was ultimately the provocation for creating a workable social universe. Ritual processes bring the world into order and completeness.

Certain African cosmogonic myths contain tropes familiar to Jews and Christians, such as the consumption of forbidden fruits. The Basari (Northern Togo and Northern Ghana) creation myth speaks of a creator god named Unumbotte who makes man, a snake, and an antelope; he then places them on unrefined earth with one tree. Unumbotte gives them seeds to plant, and one produces a tree that bears red fruit. The creator god eats these fruits without offering any to the human, the antelope, or the snake. The snake convinces the human and the antelope to eat the fruits. Unumbotte is surprised to find that they have done so but does not punish them for it. Rather, the antelope gets to live out its days eating grass, as it prefers. Human beings received new food from the Creator: yams, sorghum, and millet. The narrative says the humans ate in groups around separate bowls and that was the beginning of different languages forming on earth. The snake received venom from the Creator, with which he strikes humans and animals, often leading to their deaths.

Though similar to the Genesis story, this myth has a very different resolution and moral valence. The story establishes how human, animal, and agricultural life came about. Unlike the Genesis story, where God punishes Adam and Eve for eating the forbidden fruit, Unumbotte spares the human and the animals for their disobedience but gives them separate ways of life. Cultural diversity, exemplified by the various languages, is also featured in the Basari narrative. Although this part of the story explains the same phenomenon as does the story of the tower of Babel—namely, that people speak many different languages—the moral valence is again very different. In the story of the tower of Babel, found in the book of Genesis, the multiplicity of languages is a punishment from God for humankind's pride. The Basari myth, on the other hand, does not assign any sense of blame or wrongdoing; people simply speak different languages because they divided into smaller groups.

African oral narratives also include myths of origin, which explain an ethnic group's foundation and traditions. Among the Maasai of Kenya, some believe that the ethnic group's clans descend directly from the creator god and his two wives. The first wife received red cattle upon marriage and established her home on the righthand side of the gate. The second received black cattle and built her house on the gate's left side. The first wife birthed three boys: Lelian, who founded the Ilmolelian clan; Lokesen, father of the Imakesen clan; and Losero, progenitor of the Iltaarrosero. These forefathers built their homes on the right side, like their mother, and their descendants formed the righthand clans. The second wife also birthed sons who founded their own clans: Laiser established the Aiser clan; Lukum planted the Lukumai clan. Like their forefathers who constructed their dwellings on the lefthand side, they are clans of the left hand.

While myths may explain clan distinctions, it is not unusual for African narratives to inform us about tribal origins worldwide. The Nkundo from the Democratic Republic of Congo tell an extensive tale about tribal origins throughout the earth. The central component is a mother, Mbombe, who births numerous children. Jibanza, in particular, was born as an adult warrior and avenges his father's death. During his escapades, he manages to collect several warriors and people from other groups into his family. For instance, instead of killing one of his rivals, his sister weds this enemy, thereby creating an alliance between the two groups. Jibanza becomes king after receiving divine approval from Elima, the god of heaven. As he returns home, he deposits people in different locations and assigns them their ethnic group's name. Albert De Rop, the researcher who collected this story, notes that when European people are in the audience, the narrator will add that Jibanza traveled across the sea and deposited people on all the continents. This is an effort to explain the presence of non-black people on Earth and to make the story as inclusive as possible. African storytellers have always been curious about European researchers who wanted to interview them about their trade. By being inclusive, the storytellers convey how the interviewers are part of the cosmogony.

Some African myths not only explain the origin of different races but also attempt to account for the storyteller's and audience's perception that blacks were shorted in their allotment from the Creator when compared with whites. Many of these stories revolve around the actions of a white man and a black man that God makes as the first humans. In nearly every case in this genre, because of some foolish action on the part of the black man, the white man gets the better apportionment—whether it is guns or literacy or greater wealth—while the black man is left with scraps, morsels, some lesser gift, or is cursed with hard labor. Such stories are so widespread throughout Africa, and frequently appear so soon after first contact, that they must be more than merely an internalization of white racism. Michael D. Jackson's interpretation gets to the heart of an understanding of myth as an attempt to create meaning, rather than accept things as they lie. Jackson writes: "With myths, people actively work on the world, molding and reshaping it in terms of the exigencies of their everyday lives." In particular, Jackson strikes on the fact that, in this genre, it is almost always the actions of the black man that generate negative consequences. As such, the myth perceives blacks as agents rather than simply the victims of a random fate that they had no role in shaping. Additionally, Jackson highlights the exaggerated, comedic aspects of these stories, which invite the audience to laugh at the absurdities of a situation that otherwise could only be construed as tragedy.

Myths pertaining to ethnic or racial origin often go hand in hand with migration myths. The aforementioned Maasai tell a migration myth that speaks about the Ilarinkon, who inhabited their current territory prior to the Maasai migration into the area. The Ilarinkon were impatient with the Maasai's presence and encouraged them to leave. The bountiful land, however, was too comfortable for the Maasai, and they refused to move. A most formidable man led the Ilarinok and, according to myth, the Maasai defeated him only by outsmarting him with clever responses to his seemingly impossible requests. When the opponent requested a sandal with hair on both sides, a witty Maasai boy instructed his elders to cut off the ear of a mule and make a sandal with it, since this portion of animal skin would have hair on both sides. Tricks such as this continued until the clever boy came close enough to the Ilarinkon leader to kill him, thereby enabling the Maasai to conquer this group and officially control their land. The story resembles the David and Goliath narrative, in that a physically gigantic and militarily sophisticated opponent succumbs to the attack from a miniature, less-equipped foe. It thus points out the various conflicts and communal clashes that occurred between aboriginal settlers and invaders who often succeed in conquering the other and taking their land. Such narratives are common in African communities.

Sadly, such myths are sometimes used to justify political violence, oppression, and atrocities. In Rwanda, Hutu historical myths were used to justify acts of genocide against the Tutsi people, a powerful ethnic minority with whom they had lived peacefully for centuries. The Hutu, predominantly farmers, see themselves as the autochthonous inhabitants of that region, having arrived millennia ago during a major wave of Bantu migration. The Tutsi, who originated in the Nile region, are predominantly pastoralists, and arrived sometime after the Hutu. In their myths, the Hutu tell of how the Tutsi defrauded them of the land by tricking them into servitude in exchange for products derived from cattle. Other stories tell of how the Tutsi subdued the Hutu under a Tutsi monarch, supplanting a less formal Hutu leader. Read through the lens of these myths, the Hutu welcomed Belgian colonial rule because they were given equal opportunities to succeed; by contrast, independence was seen as bringing an unwelcome reversion to a prior state of servitude to Tutsi overlords. These myths not only provided a ready language for those who wished to incite ethnic violence against the Tutsi—offering a way to justify it as a long-delayed struggle for freedom against invasive tyrants—but also allowed those caught up in gang violence to contextualize their actions after the fact.

A similar process can be seen in play in Darfur, Sudan. Events in the Sudan remind one that not all myths are ancient, and that a relatively recent historical myth can still exert enormous power over events and people's imaginations. In the Sudan, myths of origin have been used to justify genocide and systematic cruelty. The Sudan is predominantly governed by northern Muslims whose own fairly recent myth of origin proposes that they are the descendents of Arabian warlords from the north. Therefore, they see themselves as being ethnically distinct from the southern, predominantly Christian population, which is identified by these "Arabs" as black. This is in spite of the fact that the two populations are phenotypically identical, and in the face of strong evidence that Sudanese northerners have no more claim to Arab descent than their southern neighbors. While the international press has often focused on the Darfur genocide as an example of religious violence—of Muslims against Christians—the Sudanese themselves understand it principally as an issue of race. On the surface, this is baffling to the observer, unless one is familiar with the myth of origin that is the source for this claim.

The Dama of Namibia have a migration story that claims their ethnic group began when a pregnant woman and her daughter parted from their caravan while wandering through the desert. The woman encountered a cannibal witch who assisted in the birth of her twins. The witch ate the woman while her daughter went to fetch water. Since the girl and the twin boys were alone, they grew up in the witch's house. One day, they trapped the witch in her house and set the structure on fire. They demanded that the witch return their mother's heart and, upon receiving it, buried it in the ashes. The mother then reincarnated and married the first twin, giving the second to her daughter as a husband. The mountain-dwelling High Dama descended from the first couple and the Low Dama of the plains originated with the latter pair. This story of incest and cannibalism poses several puzzles to us. It explains the origin of human life in mystical and magical terms. The witch is an important element of African society and plays a central role in bringing about a human community. It is interesting that until the heart of the woman was properly buried, the children did not rest, and indeed the proper burial leads to the reincarnation of the deceased mother. It is their belief that without proper burial the dead will become a menace to the living. Moreover, the heart as a central organ of the body deserves a peaceful rest after death.

Explanation for the origin of death is as important as the creation of the cosmos. According to the Maasai, death entered the world when the first human male, Leeyio, mispronounced a decree the Creator instructed him to declare over the corpse of anyone who dies: "Man die and come back again. Moon die and stay away." He had inverted this decree and consequently allowed death to enter the world. Interestingly, the first person to die was his neighbor's child. Leeyio's careless speech over the child's body prevented his own child from coming back to life when he passed away. The story seems to suggest that people must attend carefully to their neighbors' well-being, because another person's troubles may also befall you; the carelessness demonstrated toward others may cause you trouble.

Many stories about the origin of death revolve around some mistake on the part of an early human ancestor, or else on the part of a semidivine messenger. In most cases, humans are originally made by the divine to be deathless—a theme found also in the book of Genesis. This addresses one of the central concerns of almost all religions, that of the origin of evil in the world and whether God is infinitely good. If horrible things, such as death, befall us in the course of our natural lives, does it not mean that the creator intended these things and is therefore evil? In these stories of the origin of death, however, it is clearly shown that suffering and death came to be against the intentions of God—either by some mistake or because of human error.

A theme common among myths about death's origins is the confused messenger. The Xhosa tale (South Africa) says Qamata, the supreme being, sent Chameleon to Earth to deliver a message to human beings. Chameleon was to inform human beings that they would not die. At some point in his journey, he became tired and slept. Upon waking, he found Lizard, who inquired about his mission. Lizard then ran off and told the humans they would die. Despite the Chameleon's attempt to correct the statement, the humans believed the lizard. For the Chagga of Kenya, death resulted not from an errant decree but from violated secrecy. The Chagga claim death entered the world when a hungry stranger encountered the community and ate the yams Ruwa had forbidden the people to eat. Ruwa punished the elder with death and blindness. After much supplication from a minister of Ruwa, the supreme being healed him and told him the people would no longer die. Rather, when the time came, they would shed their skin and receive a new one. In order for the transformation to succeed, however, the elder must shed his skin in secret. In this he failed because his granddaughter, commissioned to care for him, returned too soon and caught him in the process. Thus, the elder died, and now all humanity undergoes death.

Epics about cultural heroes are another important type of myth. Cultural heroes are frequently the subject of a culture's most important myths—one prime biblical example being Moses. Cultural heroes frequently blur the lines between human, animal, god, ancestor, and spirit, and often play key roles in cosmogonic myths and in myths of migration. In some cases, cultural heroes mirror deities and function as creator gods. Most often, they are endowed with, or invent, essential abilities like hunting or farming. Such figures usually do not belong to a particular lineage but rather to the people as a whole, although in some cases, they are the founders of particular lineages, clans, and ethnic groups. The category includes humans who were warriors or performed astounding deeds, warranting their immortalization in cultural memory. Cultural heroes are also often kings or rulers, and their stories will relate the founding of a line of kings, a royal house, or a territory. During festivals and rituals, the community may narrativize these events. Epics are often connected with cultural heroes, like Kankan Musa, the Malian king who laid the foundation of one of the largest medieval gold-rich empires in Western Sudan. They are important in religion because they continue to provide the sacred canopy that legitimizes and sacrilizes the identity of their people. During annual festivals, the community gathers from different places to remember ancestors by participating in reenactments of primordial events. For this reason, cultural heroes can also serve as the basis of what has often been called civil religion—that is, a set of secular narratives, rituals, and beliefs that unite a people under a banner of cultural and national identity.

The Mbuti pygmies of Congo's Ituri rainforest have a myth attributing their culture's creation to Aparofandza, a primordial being who birthed them and taught them hunting and procreation. Other narratives depict the chameleon as a cultural hero who becomes Owner of All Things after successfully bringing Lightning's anvil to a mountain top. Myth surrounding Kintu, a Baganda (Uganda) cultural hero, suggests he was both a primordial being and an ancestor. As the first man, he functions as the Baganda progenitor. His quest to marry Nambi, daughter of Gulu, king of Heaven, positions him as a trickster character who outsmarts the gods and establishes Baganda people on earth. Thus, titling him a "cultural hero" points to his success as the founder of a culture and his ability to surmount impossible odds.

For the Yorùbá of Nigeria, many of the *òrìṣà*, the traditional gods, blur the line between divinities and cultural heroes. The goddess Ọ̀sun in Òṣogbo, Southern Nigeria, is also a cultural hero associated with the founding of certain territories and is honored in some cases as a war hero. The god Ṣàngó is another example; now honored as a god, he was also a historical person, the third Aláafin (ruler) of the Ọ̀yọ́ Empire, the largest ancient empire in southwestern Nigeria from the seventeenth to nineteenth centuries. Oramiyan is regarded as the builder of Ifẹ̀ and the founder of Ọ̀yọ́. The *òrìṣà* Odùduwà played a vital role in the creation of the universe but is also honored as the first Yorùbá ruler and founder of the Yorùbá race. The *Ọọni*, the Yorùbá high king, is seen as a living embodiment of Odùduwà, but all Yorùbá royal houses—and all Yorùbá people—trace their lineage back to Odùduwà. Thus, Odùduwà is treated as both a divine spirit and an ancestor.

These mythical figures are all examples of cultural heroes because they are celebrated as playing key roles in the establishment of Yorùbá culture; moreover they are often honored as having been living people. They constitute a separate yet interrelated category in the pantheon of gods. Other cultural heroes, such as the great Zulu leader Shaka Zulu, have not been deified but are still venerated as ancestors. This provides an important perspective on gods, ancestors, and spirit beings, and while these are useful categories of analysis, in practice the distinctions are often not clear-cut.

Chapter 2
Gods, ancestors, and spirit beings

In African indigenous religions, the principal deities, spirits, gods, ancestors, and personal and impersonal forces are regarded as active agents in the created world, with theistic and nontheistic notions of supernatural forces embedded in the various cosmologies. African pantheons of gods, goddesses, spirits, and other nonhuman beings are varied in number and complex in character. Deities inhabit a world primarily created for humans, and they exert extraordinary influence over day-to-day human affairs. These pantheons often bear a collective name. Among the Yorùbá of Nigeria, it is òrìṣà, and the Baganda of Uganda call it *baalubale*. In practice, however, it is most common to find individuals and families committed to relationships of reciprocity with a smaller subset of spirits and ancestors, to whom they offer service and in return can expect assistance in times of need. While there may be hundreds of òrìṣà—a traditional number of 201 or 401 is often given—an individual will often only actively serve several or even just one. The spirits an individual serves are often inherited from one's family and place of birth. Elaborate mythological narratives elucidate significant clues to the divinities' habits, functions, powers, activities, and influence. The character of divinities will give expression to core cultural beliefs, and people will often reference how divinities are illustrative of both good and bad ideals. Stories across the continent depict the deities as anthropomorphic beings or impersonal spirits who share numerous characteristics with their human devotees. Gods and spirits are made in the image of humans. They speak, are heard, endure punishment, and attain rewards just like human beings.

The relationship between the many gods and the Supreme God varies from region to region, from people to people. Some African cosmogonies envision the Supreme God as the highest and most powerful being, prior to everything else and of unknown origins or self-genesis. A remote or absent creator god is a common trope in African creation stories. Narratives from Nigeria to Zimbabwe depict an original deity who observes the creative process rather than participating in it directly, leaving the generation and continued maintenance of the world to lesser divinities. It is common to see such a god as being far removed from human affairs; for this reason, lesser deities are instead regularly petitioned for succor.

Some groups regard the Supreme God as co-equal with the deities, as the first among equals, or as a king among chiefs. The complex interconnectivity between the Supreme God and the lesser divinities makes African religions difficult to classify as either monotheistic or polytheistic. One could argue that such a binary remains irrelevant in the African context. Such debates began with the influence of Islam and Christianity. Nevertheless, scholars have noted that the expansion of scale from microcosm to macrocosm introduced by Islam and Christianity brought the once remote—yet present—Supreme God to the fore. Notably, it is often the case that, in areas that have a long history of Islam, adherents of African traditional religions will use a word for their Supreme God that is derived from Islam. For example, the Kuranko people of Sierra Leone, many of whom maintain at least some of their traditional religious practices, use the name "Altala" (derived from the Arabic "Allah") for their version of the supreme divinity. This is a clear marker of how African traditional religions, Islam, and Christianity have had clear impacts on one another, often hybridizing rather than simply obliterating the competition.

The term "Supreme God" is a peculiar use of the word "god." In numerous African ethnic groups, the ultimate deity is considered a supernatural being much like those associated with natural phenomena, only larger. It remains difficult to translate concepts such as the Yorùbá òrìṣà agbaye into English. At best, this title references two complementary theistic notions. First, the term means "universal god," a god who is associated with the entire world rather than pinned to one particular location. A second interpretation renders òrìṣà agbaye as "god of the universe." Both concepts suggest that this entity is "supreme" in that its stewardship extends over and throughout the earth.

The Supreme Being remains the most significant superhuman entity in African religions, despite the fact that, in practical matters, emphasis is placed on seeking assistance from other deities. This is because the Supreme Being is usually seen as the engineer of fate and therefore, in a sense, the originator of causality. While other deities and spirits can intervene in the course of events, it is the Supreme Being that ultimately determines their outcome. The premier deity may also be seen as a divine principle embodying the idea of life, abundance, and the blessings of human procreation and agricultural fertility. Some cultures see the Supreme Being as male, others female, and in other cases as hermaphroditic, androgynous, or without gender. Several cultures, such as the Fon of Benin Republic, believe in a twin entity and emphasize the cooperation between male and female that is necessary for creation to occur. Androgynous notions of the Supreme God suggest that equilibrium in the cosmos depends on a balance between equal and opposite forces.

The Fon of Benin Republic believe that Mawu-Lisa, the twin couple descending from the Supreme Being (Nana Buluku), gave birth to seven pairs of twins. These new pairs became the central deities in the Voodoo pantheon. Mawu-Lisa once called the children together to distribute their inheritances. The eldest pair, Sakpata, received Earth to govern. The storm twins, Heviosso,

22

gained control over thunder and lightning. Jurisdiction over the production of iron implements belongs to Ogu, the twins that represent iron. They were the most mighty set of twins and were supplicated to clear paths through forests, cultivate land, and to make tools for hunting and farming. Mawu-Lisa also gave each divinity a unique language with which to communicate with one another, a language shared only with their respective priests and priestesses. According to the same myth, Legba, the youngest deity, attained fluency in all the languages of the gods. This skill enables Legba to facilitate communication between the divinities.

The Supreme God looms large in many narratives and myths that convey the nature of African cosmologies, though not in the same way as in Islam and Christianity, which now dominate African worldviews and social life. Nevertheless, in their African forms, these two monotheistic traditions borrow heavily from the indigenous traditions they have encountered. I recently attended a church service during which a Nigerian pastor invoked the Supreme God by calling out in Yorùbá what he termed the beautiful names of the highest deity. Many of these honorific names I recognized to be from Ifá divination poetry, a traditional form of Yorùbá divination. This may also have been partly inspired by how, in Islam, God (Allah) has ninety-nine praise names that describe his many attributes.

The Supreme Being as a force among us

For the Lango of Uganda, the Supreme Being, called Jok, is more like a Supreme Force. Jok is as intangible, invisible, indivisible, and ubiquitous as the wind and tends to inhabit trees, hills, and mountains. It may be of either gender. The Lango describe Jok as benevolent and as a creator who generated the cosmos, Earth, and the rainy and dry seasons. Unlike other African cultures in which the Supreme God is generally seen as an invisible and remote deity, the Lango people may access Jok directly through prayers and divination. As with divinities the world over, Jok tends to punish those who neglect or disobey it. Lango people know this deity in several manifestations, the oldest being Atida. Also known as Min Jok, meaning "mother of god," she is associated with hunting, fighting, and rain. Her oracles are primarily tended by women, and large banyan trees are sacred to her.

Another emanation is Jok Adongo, associated with the cult of trees and the connection the Lango make between trees and rainmaking. Though invisible and intangible, it is said that Jok Lango, another manifestation of Jok, speaks Lango and carries a shield and two spears. It is the Jok of illnesses. Other important manifestations include Jok Nam, the force of the river, and Jok Orongo, who manages the souls of human beings and from whom the soul originates. The emergence of certain Joks can actually be dated, as with Jok Omarari, who first appeared in 1916 as the deity of the bubonic plague. This gives some sense of how religious change regularly occurs in response to the changing needs of a society.

Despite the differences between them, all the Jok entities overlap. Driberg refers to Jok as a "Spiritual Force composed of innumerable spirits, any of which may be temporarily detached without diminishing the oneness of the Force." It is clear from Lango narratives that gods and spirits derive many of their attributes from the physical landscape and natural phenomena specific to a community's particular place and space.

The Luo of Kenya hold religious beliefs similar to those of the Lango of Uganda. They believe in a Supreme Being called Nyasaye and in a spiritual force called Juok. Nyasaye may be understood as androgynous, because some appellations refer to the god as female and others as male. In either case, Nyasaye is the origin of life and created the cosmos, Earth, and all living beings. Some myths depict the creator forming human and animal life in the same manner that a potter molds clay. Nyasaye is omniscient and omnipresent, unknowable and untouchable, too close to feel and too far to reach. It provides children, wealth, good health, and agricultural bounty. Since these things belong to it, the divinity

24

1. The Gèlèdé masking tradition of the Yorùbá of southwestern Nigeria celebrates the mystical power of the sacred mothers, known as *awon ìyá*. This ceremony serves to propitiate and appease what the community believes to be the benevolent and destructive powers of these sacred mother figures.

may also take them away. Some Luo pray directly to this Supreme Being and address it as "father," but most Luo pray instead only to their ancestors. For the Luo, Juok is a spiritual power residing in all living and nonliving things. It is often identified with wind or air and consists of spirits, souls, shadows, and ghosts. It evinces itself in living creatures, dreams, visions, and natural phenomena.

The Sotho-Tswana of South Africa have an intricate notion of god similar to that of the Lango. According to Gabriel M. Setiloane, Modimo (the Supreme Being) is intangible and genderless. Its primary manifestation is as the numinous sky, and as a consequence it is associated with the direction of "above." Modimo is a singular Supreme Entity whose presence infuses all things but is not perceived directly through the senses. Modimo is the source of all, a self-generating entity that enables creation to emerge. The Sotho-Tswana also refer to Modimo as mother, noting the nurturing that it provides. This does not seem to gender this supernatural force but rather describes the tenderness it has for human beings. This entity also extends goodness to human beings and embodies justice. Ultimately, Modimo is everywhere and extends into every realm of life.

There are other African cultures, which also believe in a mystical force that suffuses all things, but do not necessarily divinize this force or associate it intimately with a Supreme Being. For example, the Yorùbá have the concept of *àṣẹ*, loosely translated as "force" or "power." *Àṣẹ* suffuses all living things, many features of the natural world, and ritual objects. Divinities as well as people use and shape *àṣẹ* in order to enact their will. However, *àṣẹ* itself is morally neutral. It is perhaps best likened to electricity, which powers so much of our world and gives life to things, yet is itself not a conscious entity with any feelings about how and when it is used.

The Supreme Being as distant creator

Akan cosmology (Ghana) envisions a distant, male creator—Nana Nyame—who alone remains responsible for the cosmos and the earth. Southern Akan posit that he finished creating the earth on a Friday, while northern Akan claim he concluded one day earlier. It is taboo for farmers from each location to work the land on these respective days. It is said that Nana Nyame has knowledge of everything. A myth teaches that Nyame lives in the sky, which at some point was close enough for humans to touch. In one myth, Nyame was formerly close enough to be constantly poked by the pestle of a woman who was pounding *fufu*, a staple food that is made by pounding cooked yam. Consequently, Nana Nyame distanced himself from the world in order to escape the aggravation.

In a narrative from the West African country of Mali, Amma, the Dogon creator god, is male and breaches the order of the universe by impregnating the earth. Earth, here, is female and Amma's creation. Amma is considered all-powerful, yet also the reason why the world began awry. Later, Amma and the earth produced Nommo, divine reptilian water spirits who played an important role in forming human beings. Since life developed from water, and since the vital fluid manifests in living things, the Dogon consider the Nommo generative of all life forms.

The Lozi of Zambia's Supreme Being, Nyambe, created his wife, Nasilele, and the first human being, Kamunu. The sun symbolizes this Supreme Being and, in contrast, the moon represents his wife. The creator once lived on Earth with Nasilele, but departed to the sky when Kamunu and his wife continued to copy his genius (i.e., creating tools, hunting, and carpentry). It is said that Nyambe is progenitor of the Lozi royal families. At the same time, Lozi autochthonous belief suggests that he can cause human misery: he can be quick to anger, vindictive, and resentful. Nyambe remains distant and uninterested in human affairs.

For the Yorùbá, the Supreme Being is a sky god called Olódùmarè (sometimes called Ọlọ́run). Olódùmarè created the entire universe but operates on it somewhat removed, in a way that is reminiscent of Western Deist theology of God as a clockmaker. When it came time to actually create life on Earth, Olódùmarè directed the council of divine spirits called *òrìṣà* to descend to the earth under the leadership of the eldest *òrìṣà* Ọbàtálá. Olódùmarè gave to Ọbàtálá all of the tools they would need to create land and life but did not participate in the act of creation itself. Although the course of fate ultimately lies in the hands of Olódùmarè, he (or she, or it, or they) do not directly intervene in the course of events. Therefore, adherents of Yorùbá traditional religion address their supplications and prayers to the *òrìṣà* who brought life to the earth and continue to be invested in what happens there.

Ancestors

Ancestral tradition, the veneration of deceased parents and forebears, constitutes a key aspect of African religions. Some traditions regard ancestors as equal if not superior to the deities within the pantheon; also, it is not always easy to make a distinction between ancestors and divinities. Other traditions centralize ancestral veneration, because it remains instrumental to lineage, clan, and family formations. Ancestors, having transcended the human realm, occupy a higher realm of existence and are equipped to bestow honor and blessings on the living members of their lineage. A reciprocal relationship links the living and the dead. Ritual offerings are given in exchange for blessings from the ancestors. Conversely, neglect of a lineage's ancestors can lead to misfortune, illness, and even death.

A prime example of the intimate interaction between the living and the ancestors is the involvement of the ancestors in rites of passage for the living, such as naming, puberty, marriage, and death. This transition cannot be successfully accomplished without the assistance and support of the ancestors, since evil forces, personified as malevolent spirits and particulary as witches, could otherwise disrupt the event and adversely affect the continued existence of human life and the cosmic order. The blessing of the ancestors wards off these disruptive forces and thus guarantees success.

Some African societies delineate between ancestors who lived during recent memory and those who died more than four generations ago. For the Ovambo people of northern Namibia, a distinction exists between "ancestors" and the "living dead." The former (*aathithi*) refer to the "forgotten deceased," those whose activities and memory cannot be recalled by the living members of their lineages. The living dead, on the other hand, are the recently deceased. The Ovambo further separate deceased relatives (*oohe nooyina*), regarded as those constituting one's living dead, and the living dead of all other bloodlines. While the deceased relatives command respect and attention, the ancestors of others are virtually unacknowledged, a tradition that highlights the imperative of maintaining a direct genealogical link with one's recently deceased ancestors.

Several African cosmologies envision an ancestral realm similar to the human realm. For some cultures, this means the afterlife involves the pursuit of plenty. A proverb among the Yorùbá says, "If the land of the ancestors is full of gold and diamonds, they will not return to the human community to solicit gifts." The proverb explains the reciprocal relationship between the living and the dead, while also emphasizing the ancestors' human qualities. Importantly, this proverb emphasizes that the forebearers need their progeny in order to sustain themselves in the afterlife just as much as the living need blessings, wisdom, and grace from their predecessors. The living and the ancestors depend upon one another for survival. In contrast, the Kono of Sierra Leone believe that the ancestors' world contains greater beauty and prosperity than the human one. The society of the dead, nevertheless, mirrors the society of the living. Families and clans live separately in the afterlife, and the heads of lineages constitute the council of ancestral spirit elders. In the afterlife, ancestors possess power and authority unparalleled by living elders, thereby validating their social and moral control over their progeny. Although still close to humanity, ancestors mostly cast aside negative individual characteristics that they had while incarnate, becoming ideal men and women able to counsel the living on their social and moral interactions. After death, the dead assume a perfected moral personality. Although the Kono worldview includes a Supreme Being and several lesser gods, it is the ancestors who occupy first place in the people's religious practice.

The BaKongo (who reside in the Democratic Republic of Congo) and the Kaguru (from Tanzania) believe elders are closest to the ancestors. Consequently, the community's aged wield the most influence on how to interact with them. The elders determine what pleases the ancestors, whom to blame for the ancestor's discontent, and who interprets the ancestor's will. As emissaries and mediators, the elders speak for the ancestors when they intervene in and resolve conflicts. Alternately, a connection is also sometimes made between the ancestors and the newly born. For the Beng people of Côte d'Ivoire, babies are seen as reincarnated ancestors who, for the first months and years of their lives, retain many of their ancestral memories. In particular, they are still acclimated to their lives in *wrugbe*, the afterlife, which is envisioned by the Beng to be a distant European-style metropolis. In *wrugbe*, the ancestors live extremely cosmopolitan lives, speaking all human languages fluently and using European currencies to pay for their needs. Babies, because they have only recently come from *wrugbe*, are treated as though they already know all languages fluently, and parents speak to them as such— for example, explaining to them in full sentences that they mustn't cry or be difficult. Rather than learn Beng, babies are believed to gradually *forget* all other languages except for Beng. In order to make babies feel less homesick for the world of *wrugbe*, Beng give their babies gifts, such as colonial French coins (used as currency in *wrugbe*), which will make their new surroundings feel more familiar. Likewise, babies are kept away from anything that might weaken their tenuous connection to the world of the living. For this reason, they are not brought near dead bodies or cemeteries until it is determined that they are firmly grounded in their new bodies.

A critical issue in ancestral veneration is who may become an ancestor. The answer varies across the continent. Among the Manyika of Zimbabwe, only male members of the lineage receive ancestor status, because the title references male "sexual potency" (although not necessarily fatherhood). Female ancestors also exist, such as among the agricultural Ila people in central Zambia, a matrilineal society in which both men and women pour libations to their ancestresses. In some cases, only certain children with sacred births may become ancestors. The Sukuna-Nyamwezi people of Tanzania automatically deem twins as ancestors by virtue of their birth, and the care for deceased twins remains solely women's responsibility.

Regardless of who becomes an ancestor, the process for attaining the title begins with death. Among Africans, death signifies a transition from one life stage to the next. Peaceful passage is key to becoming an ancestor, and the living perform burial rites and ceremonies in order to ensure a tranquil crossing for the deceased. In some cases, the recently deceased is believed to still dwell in or around the corpse for several days, during which time family and friends will continue to talk to the person as if alive. Proper burial includes ostentatious funeral ceremonies in which all the deceased's descendants participate. Because the dead are still spiritually very much alive, the family of the living makes every effort during funeral rites to make sure that their new ancestor is pleased. For the Ga people of Ghana, one way that this is expressed is through the use of elaborate fantasy coffins in the shape of fish, birds, cars, airplanes, cell phones, and every other imaginable shape. Extremely expensive and always custom-built, these coffins are designed to flatter the deceased and reveal to the community something important about his or her station in life.

Another common requirement for a person to become an ancestor is that he or she must have died a "good death," one not caused by incurable sickness (such as leprosy, smallpox, or AIDS), an accident, or violence. Most importantly, the deceased must transition at an old age, signifying wisdom and experience. In some societies, burials and the formation of new ancestors are a time of great instability. Great anxiety, confusion, and unpredictability infiltrate the Bambara of Mali. They consider death a liminal period when the fortunes of the deceased and his or her descendants are unpredictable. Similar preoccupations consume the Yorùbá, who pray immediately against successive fatalities, thereby mitigating disturbances in the lineage.

Maintaining the lineage remains one's responsibility, whether in the human world or in the ancestral world. To this end, ancestors not only bless their progeny's fertility but they also undergo reincarnation. Although it may seem confusing, many African peoples, including the Beng, believe that a spirit can remain an ancestor even when it has also reincarnated in human form. The Lupupa people of the Democratic Republic of Congo believe that a spirit returns to be reborn in a lineage when its living descendants maintain an amicable relationship with the ancestors. The general rule holds that an individual's spirit may return in a human body only three times, usually via a grandchild. Thus newly born grandchildren often bear their forefather's or foremother's name. For the Yorùbá, ancestors are believed to reincarnate within their own lineage. While in most cases this return takes time, in other cases it is believed to happen almost instantaneously. For example, a common Yorùbá name for a son is Babatunde, meaning "father has come back." The name indicates that the child is believed to be the reincarnation of a deceased father or grandfather. This name is especially given to a son who is born after his grandfather has died. Similarly, a girl born after the death of her grandmother is named Iyabo or Yetunde. Among the Beng of Côte d'Ivoire elders spend time with their grandchildren, because they understand the infants have just emerged from the place to which the elderly will soon travel: the afterlife.

In many cases, it is difficult to draw a sharp line between ancestors and divinities. With each successive generation, the dead tend to become more abstracted as their characters shed the traces of their humanity and, like rarified jewels, an ancestor emerges. Sometimes, at some point during this process, a quantum leap occurs from ancestor to divinity. The water spirits called *simbi* are said, at least by some BaKongo people, to be ancestors who have grown old and rejuvenated themselves numerous times in the afterlife. The BaKongo believe that ancestors gradually age, and eventually shed their skin and become young again. At some point, instead of rejuvenating themselves, they slip into the water, at which time they transition to being *simbi*.

In rare cases, conditions such as an unusual birth will cause a person to become a minor divinity immediately upon death. For example, among the Yorùbá, the Fon, and many other west African cultures, human twins are considered to be divine spirits. Upon death, twins become subjects of cultic veneration related to, but distinct from, the cult of the ancestors. For the Yorùbá, it is considered extremely dangerous if one of the twins dies, leaving the pair separated by the gulf of death. It is believed that the two will attempt to be reunited unless ritual actions are taken to guarantee that the deceased twin is kept happy while the remaining twin lives out the rest of his or her natural life. This also explains why a twin statuette (ère ìbejì) commissioned by the twins' parents is carved as a living symbol and partner to the living twin. It represents his or her deceased twin.

Divinities in conflict

Today there is no place on the African continent that polytheism—that is, the worship of multiple gods—is not extremely controversial and embattled. In past centuries—and in fact, until very recently—African traditional religions were often practiced alongside Islam and Christianity. This is not to paint a too rosy picture of interreligious relations: there were certainly periods of intense religious conflict, holy war, and jihad. Nonetheless, interreligious relations in Africa today have achieved a nearly unprecedented fever pitch of intolerance, thanks in large part to the rapidly growing popularity of radical forms of Evangelical Christianity and Islam. While Muslims and Christians routinely and often violently fight with one another over control of the public sphere and people's souls, they share a common enemy in practitioners of African traditional religions. Traditional religionists are often wrongly branded as pagans, witches, and sorcerers.

As has always happened during major conversions of cultures from one religion to another, many aspects of African traditional religions have been absorbed into African Islam and Christianity. Attributes assigned by a culture to the multiple deities and spirit beings are often transferred to the one and only God of the new monotheistic faith. Ancestor veneration is often permitted to continue, sanctioned as a "cultural" rather than an expressly religious practice. The veneration of cultural heroes is frequently admitted under the same rationale. However, in a monotheistic faith, there is no place for other divinities. Therefore, African traditional gods are labeled demons and evil spirits. In some cases, their names are even used as synonyms for Satan. For example, Nigerian Muslims often use the name of the Yorùbá divinity Èṣù as a name for the devil, instead of the more conventional Arabic name Iblis (Sàtánì).

Not all challenges to polytheism have been religious. During colonial rule of Africa, practitioners of traditional religion tended to come under the fire of colonial governors who regarded traditional religion as anti-modern, anti-Western, and a likely source of volatility and revolt. The British tended to promote conversion to Christianity, in particular the Anglican faith. In some cases, the French encouraged the practice of Islam, believing it, ironically, to have less revolutionary potential than Christianity. However, almost all colonial authorities agreed that traditional religions were dangerous, and most colonial codes of law included statutes against witchcraft and superstition—both charges that could be leveled against practitioners of traditional faiths.

To a degree, colonial authorities were right to be concerned. In numerous cases, the worship of traditional divinities did in fact serve as a site of resistance against colonial rule. The worship

of one traditional divinity in Ghana provided an opportunity
to challenge and subvert colonial British rule. As described by
Jean Allman and John Parker, Tongnaab is a god of the Talensi,
a people who live predominantly in the northern savanna of
Ghana. The Talensi were known for their adamant and sometimes
violent resistance to colonial rule. The Tong Hills, where the cult
of Tongnaab is centered, also became a site for the organization
of Talensi resistance, and after it was violently raided in 1911,
the worship of Tongnaab was effectively outlawed. The British
failed to understand the true extent of the Tongnaab cult, and in
particular did not realize that the Tong Hills were home to many
Tongnaab shrines, not just one. Therefore, every time the British
would destroy one shrine, worshippers would simply move on to
another one—in a sense flaunting the inability of the British to
control their activities. Eventually, the British were forced simply
to accept the worship of the god and once again legalized religious
practices at certain shrines in order to create the appearance that
they controlled the flow of pilgrims.

In time, the cult of Tongnaab traveled south into metropolitan
Ghana, where it shifted to being predominantly concerned
with witch-finding. Once again, it was met with resistance from
colonial authorities. This "industry" of witch-finding was seen by
colonial authorities as contrary to the projects of Christianization,
modernization, and westernization. Authorities were unsure
how to proceed, however. It was not clear that these shrines were
illegal, or that they could be prosecuted for extortion. In 1930, the
colonial government finally responded by removing witchcraft
from the criminal code and thereby making witch-finding illegal.

In spite of this change of laws, one of the most important cult
leaders, Assifu, continued to practice witch-finding at his shrine.
The authorities were ineffective at shutting him down, and
his lawyers filed formal complaints that he was being unfairly
harassed. Briefs equated the work he did to modern biomedicine
and recalled that the government had previously issued licenses

to "native physicians," a license which Assifu had held. As such, Assifu's practice was said to be no different than psychiatry. In 1931, the Society of African Herbalists was founded as a professional organization of indigenous healers. In 1940, the Akyem Abuakwa State Council regularized licensing procedures for native physicians and required that anyone wishing to found "any cult" to first purchase a license. The Asante Confederacy Council soon followed suit with similar regulations. Elsewhere, particularly in the Ewe region, witch-finding cults continued to exist in tension with government and burgeoning Christian society. Many British authorities continued to regard them suspiciously as likely safe houses for "national sentiments." Nonetheless, the Asante shift from discussion of "fetishes" to "native medicine" was to have a lasting impact by framing the defense of traditional religious practices in terms that had more cultural and legal salience.

In many areas of the African continent, the spread of Islam and Christianity has been so complete that few people remain who practice any form of traditional religion. But this is not to say that people have completely forgotten former gods or have abandoned a sense of the world as being full of numerous spirits. Many converts continue to practice ancestral veneration. In some cases, spirit cults continue to persist in ways that are seen as consistent with monotheism. In almost all of Muslim West Africa, the belief in *djinn* thrives. *Djinn* are spirits that are described in the Qur'an as having been made from fire by Allah. In many cases, they are seen as being outright evil; in other cases, they have the character of tricksters, not necessarily evil but amoral and capable of doing great harm. *Djinn* usually live in wild places and are closely associated with the powers of nature and magic. For the stout of heart, the *djinn* can sometimes be a source of talent and power, and there are numerous stories from West Africa of people being given remarkable abilities by *djinn*. Perhaps one of the most famous of such stories relates to the origin of the kora, the West African harp. The Mande people, who live in numerous countries including Senegal and Mali, credit the origin of the kora to a cultural hero named Wuleng. According to legend, Wuleng discovered a *djinn* playing the kora in the woods and asked the *djinn* to teach him how to play the instrument. The *djinn* bargained lessons in exchange for Wuleng marrying his daughter and staying in the spirit world forever. However, Wuleng was eventually able to escape his bargain and returned to share the music of the kora with the Mande people.

Legends aside, there are also *djinn*-related spirit cults found throughout western and northern Africa. Interestingly, they are typically led by women and have almost exclusively female congregations. This suggests that they provide a vital arena for female religious experience within a religious culture that is generally male-centered. These cults practice forms of ecstatic dance that seek to channel the powers of *djinn*. Although these cults are considered taboo, their popularity attests to a need that they fulfill. Even for those who do not engage in such practices, the belief in *djinn* is nearly universal in Africa, and it is considered within the range of normal to seek the help of a *marabout*—a kind of mystical, ascetic Muslim saint—in exorcising a *djinn* or mitigating its evil influence. Such insights not only provide an important view of the state of traditional religions in Africa but also offer a more nuanced understanding of Islam and Christianity as practiced in Africa. As living religions, they are all constantly in interaction with one another and changing to meet the needs of their congregants.

Chapter 3
Sacred authority: divine kingship, priests, and diviners

Sacred authority in Africa differs from stereotypical Western notions of secular leadership insofar as African monarchs, chiefs, and elders fulfill both political and religious roles. The much-vaunted Western division between religion and the body politic is often more legal fiction than reality. To give only one example, American politicians in recent decades have turned more and more to religious language to justify their political activities. In fact, for much of the history of the Western world, religion and politics have been mingled freely. Until only recently, European views of kingship have closely resembled African models, with belief in a divinely appointed king. In some cases, European kings continue to fulfill religious roles. The queen of England is both the head of the secular government and also the titular head of the Church of England. Likewise, leaders in African traditional systems impact secular and religious wisdom and guidance to their subjects, while also being custodians and guardians of religious centers such as shrines, temples, and sacred forests.

In some cases, kings are also said to possess mystical, life-sustaining powers, with their own well-being intimately entwined with the well-being of their people, lands, and institutions. For this reason, African kings are often the subject of extremely strict taboos that address how their person can be treated, predicated on an indexical relationship between the body of the king and the body of the kingdom. The Ọọni of Ifẹ̀, the highest king of the Yorùbá people, is also considered to be the embodiment of *òrìṣà* on Earth, and his health is intimately tied to the well-being of all Yorùbá people. Because of his elevated status, he cannot be addressed directly. He cannot be seen by casual onlookers to be engaging in many ordinary human activities, such as eating, nor can it be acknowledged if he is ill or has died. Numerous elaborate euphemisms are used to discuss his earthly, physical needs and body. Although the current Ọọni is more modern than many of his predecessors, he still spends much of his time within his palace compound, where the days are ordered around local judicial matters, functions, and ritual requirements and actions.

The high king of the Asante people of Ghana, the Asantehene, shares many of these same taboos. He speaks and is spoken to through the triangulations of a high-ranking attendant. Because his physical health is mystically connected to that of the Asante kingdom, it cannot be acknowledged if he succumbs to any earthly frailness. If he sneezes, all of his ministers at court will sneeze simultaneously, thereby ritually denying that the Asantehene sneezed and claiming that it was only they who did so.

Nilotic groups in southeastern Sudan associate disasters with their king and placate him for peace. According to Simon Simonse, the king's anger with the people results in drought, crop failure, and disease. Consequently, the people placate their monarch, the *ohobu lohuju* ("king of Rain"), to pardon them and release the divine energy that guarantees abundant rain for the fields and livestock. The king uses rainstones, multicolored shards of stones such as quartz, to alter the weather. While the monarch's power remains the most revered, clan leaders also possess important abilities. The Master of Worms, the Master of Winds, and the Master of Locusts are responsible for permitting or preventing these elements from disturbing the community. Similarly, the Master of Grain sanctions consumption of new crops. As the equivalent of a Minister in some modern-day state structures, these officeholders are in charge of the various portfolios, which when collectively maintained guarantee good governance, peaceful coexistence, and economic prosperity for the people.

The Nyamwezi of Tanzania also associate rain and drought with their king. Indeed, the king's body is seen as an extension of the earth itself. The king's healthy relationship with the ancestors insures adequate rainfall. If the initial ritual sacrifices do not alter the weather, then the king is beaten to tears. His tears, according to the Nyamwezi traditional worldview, will invoke the other waters in the sky, which the ancestors ultimately control. Indigenous groups in the Kafa highlands in southwest Ethiopia, such as the Kafa, Seka, and Bosa, relate their king's body to the cosmos. His physical body, it is assumed, embodies the physical well-being of the group. Specifically, the king is a second sun. The king eats only after sunset, because a meal during the day would suggest two suns present simultaneously. Eating after sunset also implies that the sun is rejuvenating its energy to rise the following day. In contrast to the ọba (king) of Benin kingdom in Nigeria, whose health embodies the entire kingdom's well-being, the ọba (the Èwí) in Adó Èkìtì, Nigeria, is not only directly linked with his town's welfare, but also this ọba intercedes for blessings from the gods and shares them with the community.

Sharp separations between different types of sacred authorities become difficult to maintain because such persons often absorb more than one responsibility. A priest can be a diviner, a king may be a prophet, a seer may be a priest, and a prophet may be a seer and diviner. Each role serves a unique yet interrelated function. Spirit mediums, members of a family or clan who are responsible for communication between humans and the gods or ancestors, are among the most powerful religious leaders. Likewise, diviners are vital for communicating with the spirit world. As examples of divinatory practice from around the continent reveal, diviners act as intermediaries between the supernatural and the human worlds. They decipher hidden meanings in order to address

2. The late Ọọni of Ifẹ̀, Sir Adesoji Aderemi, during the Olojo festival and celebration in Ilé-Ifẹ̀, Nigeria. Olojo is the festival of the sacred kingship of the Yorùbá-speaking people of Nigeria.

misfortune, sickness, death, and calamity, or to forecast good tidings or future occurrences. In many African worldviews, spirit beings have knowledge about the *why* behind disasters. It is the diviner's job to select appropriately from the vast sacred knowledge he or she possesses and to clarify its relevance to the client's situation.

Divination is an integral component to African religions. It grants access to sacred knowledge and exposes the causation for both positive and negative events in the community and in individual lives. Divinatory processes reveal the deities' feelings and messages to humans. Countless divinatory methods exist in African societies. Some utilize consecrated objects, which the diviner casts and interprets. Other techniques involve the diviner speaking from an altered state of consciousness through which the gods or ancestors speak. They include intricate tools, vast oral repertoires, and worldviews characterizing divination systems in Africa.

Mediumistic divination

Mediumistic divination refers to forms of divination involving a priest, diviner, or traditional healer who enters directly into communication with the spirit world in order to access and deliver secret knowledge to the client. Research among the Sukuma in northwest Tanzania concludes that mediumistic divination involves spirit possession, the agency of the human's spirit, and the reception of unforetold knowledge revealed either through dreams or directly from an ancestral guide who communicates with the diviner at the height of his altered state. Dreaming also functions as an altered state of consciousness for the *laibon* (diviners) of the Samburu pastoralist in Kenya. Their clairvoyance expresses itself through dreams, providing visions that enable them to know the past, present, and future. Divination among the Samburu also involves casting objects from a gourd, called *nkidong* divination. This technique requires the diviner to shake a gourd filled with numerous objects such as hyena teeth, marbles, cowries, leather knots, animal horns, glass thermometer pieces, bullets, and beads, each of which has symbolic meaning and evokes the divine energy needed to accomplish the diviner's task. A unique numerology informs the diviner's "reading" of the objects once they have been cast. He also procures meaning from the objects' configurations, noting their positions in relation to one another.

Divination among the Yaka in southwestern Democratic Republic of Congo also depends on the diviner's clairvoyance and her or his ability to identify the cause, exact time, and perpetrator of the problem that propels the client to seek consultation. Without any information from persons present, the diviner must ascertain the nature of the situation, determining whether sorcery, illness, loss, or other misfortune is to blame. In the Yaka worldview, family members, both living and dead, can impede the flow of life to an individual. The Yaka diviner will often locate the problem's source somewhere in the family tree, possibly naming a maternal great-grand-uncle as the one who holds malicious intentions. As in many African societies, there is a general belief that sorcery starts at home. A Yorùbá proverb states that although the enemy is an outsider, the messenger of the evildoer is one's relation, an insider.

Mediumistic divination in the Democratic Republic of Congo at times manifests as a cultural and religious confluence, combining Christianity with indigenous spiritual practices. A man in Matadi appointed himself the Regional Pastor for the Church of the Holy Spirit. This minister conducts healing séances with divination that utilizes several Christian practices. According to the narrative, the Church of the Holy Spirit is Protestant, but the ceremony requires the minister to wear a cassock and his female assistants wear nuns' attire. Musical selections during this event include both Catholic and Protestant evangelical hyms and serve to transport the minister into an ecstactic state. Once he begins to tremble and speak in tongues, participants know he is in trance and ready to address the client's problems. In a high-pitched, otherworldly voice, the minister channels a spirit who then tells the sick person, in KiKongo language, the source of her or his woes and the appropriate remedies.

Knowledge revealed by supernatural sources does not escape critical review by those seeking insights. Divination via spirit possession among the Nyole of Eastern Uganda often transpires as a three-way conversation between the spirits, the diviner, and the client. The diviner summons the spirits of deceased maternal great uncles with musical invocations, shaking two gourd rattles in rhythms designed to induce possession. In some cases, the spirits speak through the diviner to the client, using the diviner's mouth and body to communicate. Alternatively, the spirits may choose to speak to the diviner, who then translates the message for the client. Whereas other African ethnic groups insure the validity of the diviner's revelation by consulting someone far removed from their community whose bias is less likely to be swayed by rumor, the Nyole clients express their agreement or disagreement with the spirit's revelations during the session. Information flows back and forth between the client, the diviner, and the supernatural beings in order to arrive at the proper conclusion. Clients who are satisfied with the information provided proceed with the diviner's recommended sacrificial rites. Those who disagree strongly with the outcome may choose not to compensate the diviner and may seek guidance elsewhere.

Mediumistic divination has, at times, been met with challenges from authorities and other kinds of religious leaders who have felt that it is a dangerous, uncouth, or potentially volatile way to seek the assistance of spirits. During the early nineteenth-century reign of King Agadja of Dahomey (present-day Benin Republic), Agadja outlawed the practice of *gbo* divination, in which a priest would cause the voice of a dead relative to issue from a clay pot. He also outlawed the worship of numerous *vodun*, spirits who could be consulted by their adepts through a possessory medium. In its place, Agadja encouraged the use of Fa divination, which was imported from Yorùbáland, where it is known as Ifá. Ifá does not rely on possession but instead on a rigorously ordered system of consulting a fixed body of sacred texts. It was the opinion of King Agadja that the ordered system of Fa would present fewer potential challenges to the consolidation and centralization of his political and religious power than would the unpredictable *gbo* and *vodun* forms of divination.

Divination: devices and sacred texts

Divination devices vary in complexity throughout the continent. In some cases, the process requires only a halved kola nut or four cowry shells. Other methods employ baskets laden with myriad objects whose meanings and potential configurations the diviner must memorize. The following examples describe the tools and techniques diviners utilize to access hidden knowledge.

Ifá divination, from the Yorùbá of southwestern Nigeria, is a well-studied divination system, and this practice informs African diaspora religions throughout the Americas, including Brazilian Candomblé and Cuban Regla de Ocha (Santería). Ifá divination has also been adopted by many Yorùbá neighbors, including the Fon people of present-day Benin Republic, who know it as Fa or Afa. Ifá divination uses a divining chain (*òpèlè*) onto which nutshells are attached. The chain has four nutshells on each side. To cast the divination, the diviner (*babaláwo*, literally "father of secrets") holds the chain in the middle and throws it on his mat, making a "U" shape on the floor. Each halved nutshell will fall either concave-side up (open) or convex-side up (closed). Alternately, palm nuts may be passed from one hand to another, with the remaining number being counted. After each cast, a mark is made in the wood powder that has been spread across the divination tray. When the casting is complete, a pattern of binary data has been created on the divination tray that provides the "call number" for one of the *odù* in the Ifá corpus.

There are sixteen main *odù*, and each has sixteen subchapters, for a total of 256 possibilities. Each *odù* is a collection of poems,

3. A gathering of the senior Ifá priests of Ìlá-Ọ̀raṅgún at the Aafin of the Ọba of Ìlá-Ọ̀raṅgún in August 1982. The Ifá divination session called Ifá idagba is performed to learn what sacrifices and offerings the Ọba must make during the Orò festival to ensure that the festival will be successful.

myths, proverbs, and remedies that the diviner has memorized and from which he then commences to recite. Ifá divination poetry tends to be quite obscure and oblique, difficult to understand even for those well-versed in its cosmology. Therefore, the diviner usually must assist the client in understanding both the plain sense and the esoteric meaning of the recitations. At this stage in the process, the client identifies which oral texts seem relevant to her situation and discloses her problem. Through further questioning, the diviner then offers his final interpretation of the selected text and in the process determines the dilemma's source. Usually, the diviner prescribes a sacrificial ritual or medicinal herbal remedies to cure the client. The sacrifice can be an animal, but it can also be vegetables, a requirement to tithe, the introduction of an ascetic practice, or even religious conversion. The oral poetry (*ese ifá*) of the *odù* that is recited by the babaláwo, and which runs into unknown thousands of verses, has been the subject of much study by scholars. The corpus constitutes an encyclopedia of Yorùbá knowledge and history, touching on diverse themes and issues in human life.

A similar yet distinct divination system exists among the Ngas, Mupun, and Mwaghavul—Chadic-speaking people of the Jos Plateau in southeastern Nigeria. There are commonalities and dissimilarities between Ifá and *Pa* systems. Both systems use specific tools. *Pa* divination involves thirty river pebbles carried in a tortoise shell. It is believed that river spirits imbue these stones with the ability to reveal hidden information. Ritual cleansing and daily rinses with river water help maintain the stones' potency. The tortoise shell's significance stems from a myth wherein the tortoise hides the special stones in his shell while descending to Earth. As in Ifá, the divination process produces a binary code. After casting the pebbles, the diviner (*ngu-kos-Pa*) uses his finger to mark how many pebbles fell upon the ground. He indicates one stone by making a single indentation in a special powder. Two stones receive two strokes. Unlike Ifá divination, the Pa process requires two or more diviners: one to cast the stones and record results, and another to interpret the outcome. Rather than allow the client to select which information pertains to her or his situation, as happens in Ifá divination, Pa tradition requires the client to depart and confess her or his misdeeds to a confidant, thereby confirming the diviner's conclusions. In some cases, divinities, sorcery, or stifled anger cause one's affliction. Each case calls for specific herbal or sacrificial remedies, which the diviner prescribes.

There are several similarities between four-tablet divination, widespread among southern African groups such as the Shona and Tswana, and West African methods. The most striking similarity is that the four rectangular tablets produce one of sixteen possible configurations when cast. Each combination of face-up and face-down tablets has a specific name and corresponds to unique oral literature recited by the diviner during the consultation. A binary system undergirds this method, and each tablet bears distinct markings to identify it as senior or junior and male or female. This is not to propose that Ifá inspired four-tablet divination, or vice versa, but instead suggests that both may be related to Arabic geomancy (*'ilm al-raml*), which also uses a base-sixteen system. No conclusive research, however, has emerged on the question.

Sikidy, a complex mathematical divination system among the Sakalava of Madagascar, requires the *ombiasa* (diviner) to set up four piles of acacia tree seeds. The diviner then adds the number in the first pile together. If the number is even, he creates a new column by placing aside two seeds. If it is odd, he sets aside one seed. The *ombiasa* proceeds in this manner until he has summed all four columns, thereby producing a fifth. This technique continues until the diviner produces as many as twelve columns. Sacred knowledge informs the diviner's interpretation. In this case, each column's unique name and specific location (cardinal point and notation as either slave or prince) informs the diviner's conclusion. The Sakalava believe that a deity named Zanahary speaks to human beings through *sikidy*, enabling the seeds to reveal unknown truths. Clients and diviners use this method to understand the past, present, and future.

Whereas some divination techniques match sacred oral texts to concrete symbols, Nyole *lamuli* diviners (of eastern Africa) use Arabic-language books such as the Qur'an, the *Sa'atili Habari*, and the *Abu Mashari Faraki* directly. A three-way conversation takes place during divination: The diviner randomly selects an Arabic text and recites it to the client, then translates the passage for the client, who typically does not understand Arabic. Through this process, the text is established as an independent interlocutor in the discussion. A *lamuli*'s primary task is to explain how the randomly selected passages pertain to the client's problem. Texts selected from the *Sa'atili Habari* enable him to discern the numerology surrounding the incident. The *Abu Mashari Faraki* provides the diviner with information about the problem's cause and medicinal or ritual solution. While book divination differs greatly from the spirit possession methods common to the Nyole, both methods share a common function: to restore physical and spiritual wellness. African divination systems that reference Islamic traditions often occur in places where Islam and traditional religion have merged for centuries, often long before the introduction of Christianity. The use of the Qur'an for bibliomancy, divination through the selection of randomly selected passages, is widespread. One also finds African Christians using the Bible in a similar fashion.

While African divination practices provide some glimpses into the variety that exists, they are hardly exhaustive. In many cases, divination is extremely simple, relying less on tools and more on the spiritual talents of the individual practitioner. Mami Wata devotees in Benin Republic will sometimes use a form of water gazing to perform divination, during which the diviner— functioning more like a medium—will gaze upon the surface of a vessel of water and enter into communication with a divinity, who will divine the future. In other cases, divination may be extremely elaborate, but in a way that does not involve texts at all. The Dogon of Mali practice fox divination. As night falls, the diviner will trace an elaborate grid pattern in the sand, with each section of the grid representing different aspects of the client's or village's life. He will then recite poetry that asks the fox—sacred to the Dogon people— to come and provide an answer. In the morning, the diviner returns to examine any tracks that the fox has made across the grid during the night, and from these tracks, the answer to the problem is divined.

Witchcraft and sorcery

In opposition to those who wield sacred power for legitimate, socially sanctioned ends, there is the shadow of those who use sacred power for nefarious and selfish aims. These are the witches and sorcerers of the African world. As a beginning point, it is important to note African witchcraft is completely unrelated to the religious practices of modern neo-Pagans who sometimes use the word "Witchcraft" (or, more commonly, Wicca) as the name of their religion, sometimes self-identifying as witches. Such people practice a goddess-centered religion focused on nature veneration and holistic wellness. African views of witchcraft and sorcery bear no connection to this at all, and it is important that the reader not make the mistake of connecting them in any way.

In Africa, witchcraft is almost universally defined as the manipulation of occult forces to do harm and achieve selfish ends. Witches are typically marginal people—such as widows, the elderly, outsiders or strangers, people who isolate themselves or are unfriendly, and those whose positions in society, the village, or the lineage is tenuous. With some exceptions, witches are almost always women. Witches can cause all manner of maladies, illnesses, bad luck, misfortune, financial ruin, childlessness, failure of crops, and death. Witches rarely attack strangers, but instead focus their malevolence on people they know, especially family members. One of the most common reasons for someone to be suspected of witchcraft is if she seems to be doing inexplicably better than her neighbors. That is to say, she has a slightly nicer house, more food, her crops do better, or she has a bit of extra money. These all suggest that she may have used occult powers to steal these boons away from other people. The principal crime of witches is always antisociality; they are people in the community who secretly work against others for their own benefit.

It is not always clear whether African witchcraft beliefs describe the activities of actual people or rather describe widespread belief in something akin to boogeymen. That is to say, while there are certainly real people in Africa who seek the assistance of occult powers to do ill, many of the beliefs related to witches paint a surreal image of a creature that is not entirely human. It is commonly believed that witches can leave their bodies at night in the shape of birds and fly about doing harm, and that they can turn themselves into cars and airplanes. It is also commonly believed that they can fly during the night to distant continents but return by morning, that they can steal people's blood and reproductive fluids while they sleep, and that they eat children.

The Kgaga of South Africa believe in women with supernatural powers who inherit their dangerous abilities matrilineally. These witches, capable of transforming themselves into nocturnal animals, harm their victims with poisons that wrack the body with pain. They threaten society's normal order by decreasing the fertility of the land and the people. A major difference between witches and sorcerers is the former's use of innate powers alone, while the latter manipulates traditional medicines (such as plants and amulets). Sorcery is an indigenous technology implemented to manipulate the sacred for negative ends. Indeed, a thin line exists between healers, witches, and sorcerers. The only difference is that healers seek to generate life-sustaining outcomes while sorcerers and witches aim for destruction.

Gender distinctions among those who wield power for negative purposes vary from group to group. In the Yorùbá language, a sorcerer is called *oṣó* and a witch is called *àjẹ́*. In the Yorùbá tradition, *oṣó* is the one who practices bad medicine and uses objects or indigenous technology to manipulate the sacred, delivering harmful results to the victim. He could also use this power to acquire sudden undeserved wealth, which does not last long and often ends in the destruction of the client. Witches, *àjẹ́*, are generally women and are sometimes euphemistically called "the mothers." Contrarily, among the Bakweri of Congo, both men and women may practice *liemba*, meaning "witchcraft." A common belief in this community holds that witches kill their victims by eating their shadows. Interestingly, consumption is a common theme among African beliefs about witchcraft. The Lozi of Zambia claim that witches and sorcerers consume the flesh from their victim's cadaver in order to augment their powers. Motivations for using negative power against another person vary. The Ngas, Mupun, and Mwaghavul groups of Nigeria identify envy and intense concealed anger as the force behind negative events. For many others, it is simply the result of an inherent moral malformation.

Many African worldviews assert that power itself remains neutral until one decides how to use it. Diviners and healers tend to use power positively, while witches or sorcerers use power negatively. Yet the Tiv of central Nigeria complicate this idea by their belief that *tsav*, what Anglophone researchers translate as "witchcraft," exists in all people to some degree. Research among this group describes *tsav* as a physical substance located around an individual's heart. Tiv spiritual experts conduct autopsies in order to determine if the deceased practiced positive or negative *tsav*. Like other African ethnic groups, the Tiv believe that negative *tsav* causes unfortunate events and unlikely wealth. The opposite, however, characterizes not only diviners but also distinguished leaders and charismatic people, enabling them to enlist people's loyalty and favor. In other words, witchcraft is not simply a negative force used for malevolent means; it is also a gift innate in varying degrees within each person. Both positive and negative *tsav*, inadequately translated as "witchcraft," constitute a pillar of the Tiv moral code.

The widespread belief in witchcraft in Africa continues to puzzle scholars and outsiders. However, if one keeps in mind witchcraft is primarily an antisocial behavior that causes inexplicable gains or losses, witchcraft beliefs come into sharper focus. While using witchcraft to explain this range of phenomena may seem strange to Westerners, the explanations that Westerners offer for the same things—from derivatives to prayer—are arguably just as esoteric and shadowy. Why certain explanations prove more salient to some cultures than to others may ultimately be irreducible to a set of simple explanations. More relevant is the effect such beliefs have on the people who believe in them: Beliefs in witchcraft not only have profound effects on the personal lives of many Africans but also have significant social, economic, and political ramifications in both traditional and modern Africa. Ethnographic work among the Mura of Déla in northern Cameroon concludes that witchcraft beliefs enable women to curtail their husbands' abuse of authority. Despite men's control over resources, women manage to curtail their abuse of power by manipulating assumptions about women being capable of using witchcraft against their husbands. In effect, witchcraft beliefs enable Mura women to negotiate socioeconomic inequalities between the sexes.

While a belief in the existence of witchcraft has long been common in many African traditional societies, it has taken on new meaning in Islam and, most especially, in Christianity. Emergent Pentecostal and charismatic movements promote a Christian theology designed to stomp out the remaining vestiges of indigenous beliefs and practices. These are often identified uniformly as witchcraft—in spite of the fact that without a traditional context, most of these practices would not be considered witchcraft. In fact, traditional religious practices would be seen as the principal line of defense against witchcraft. New Christian notions not only place all traditional religious activity under the rubric of witchcraft but identify this witchcraft with Satanism, an entirely foreign concept to African worldviews. Additionally, these Christian perspectives on witchcraft subject even children to scrutiny; the youngest are not spared and can be accused of being under the influence of demonic spirits. This is a dramatic departure from traditional views of witchcraft, which typically saw children as potential victims of witchcraft, not its perpetrators. As a result of this departure from traditional views thousands of children in west and west central Africa have in recent years been cast out, beaten, abused, and killed because they were believed to be witches.

For marginalized people, witchcraft can provide both an explanation for their marginalization, and in some cases a recourse to attempt to improve their lot. In recent years, popular rumors throughout the continent have claimed that many politicians use the powers of witchcraft and sorcery to gain and help them maintain their power. Male witches who employ witchcraft in order to attain political power, and therefore become public figures, suffer less social ostricization than female witches, whose work threatens the private domain of the home. Witchcraft can also provide a compelling explanation for their seemingly unearned fortunes, monetary wealth, and invulnerability to prosecution for corruption. In other words, their successes are not simply a result of random luck or more pedestrian forms of corruption. The reason that they have succeeded in an environment where most are failing is that they are not playing fair. Instead, they are having recourse to powers that good, moral people refuse to use.

There is evidence that many marginalized people, youth in particular, are now attempting to make occult powers work to their benefit. There is a rising problem of cults operating on African university campuses. These cults are mostly filled with disenfranchised youth who are well educated but see few opportunities to improve their lives through ordinary channels. Occultism offers a seeming opportunity to improve their lot after the fashion of politicians who are also rumored to use dark forces for their own benefit. Unfortunately, these cults are also often criminal organizations, which use violence of an all-too-common sort to gain and hold power.

Themes of witchcraft have also become common in African films, in Nigerian films in particular (commonly referred to as the Nollywood film industry). These films often depict female witches who use their powers to ransom or spoil the destiny of individuals, especially relatives. In some cases, they are also portrayed as avengers of the evil perpetuated by the male elite. These films have become a ready source for a populist visual vocabulary of witchcraft and witch-hunting rituals. In these films, witchcraft often provides a too-easy explanation for the existence of evil, while also villainizing powerful women.

Witch hunts have practical underpinnings. During the late 1980s in Green Valley, Lebowa, South Africa, witch accusations and persecutions became more frequent as political and economic disenfranchisement increased among multiethnic communities. "Betterment" schemes implemented by the national government destabilized family structures and traditional chiefly authority, jeopardizing youth and leaving many agriculturalists economically dependent on a single family member's meager wage. Worse, as families from different ethnic groups coalesced into multiethnic communities, people often felt estranged and distant from one another. Anxiety, scarce resources, and political tensions fed a renewed belief in a vision of witchcraft that combined elements of Sotho, Tsonga, and Nguni traditional beliefs. Witchcraft offered an explanation not only for evil, but also the unwarranted misfortunes that befell individuals and the community.

Witch-hunting in South Africa became a means for legitimating youth agency in a culture in which only the aged traditionally possessed authority. Violence marshaled by the Brooklyn Youth Organization, one of Lebowa's political youth groups created during the late 1980s in response to injustice within the community's schools, aimed to validate young people's authority by exacting physical punishments upon accused witches who (supposedly) generated the community's misfortune. Among the reasons why witchcraft beliefs remain integral to contemporary African cultures is that they allow disenfranchised people to act against alleged agents of inequality who are within arm's reach— unlike inequality's actual agents, the politicians and shadowy global forces against whom action is typically impossible. Sacred power is typically viewed in Africa as a morally neutral force that can be used for good or evil.

Chapter 4
Ceremonies, festivals, and rituals

Ceremonies, festivals, and rituals embody, enact, and reinforce the sacred values communicated in myths. Rituals occur on calendrical cycles. They often dictate when the community honors a particular divinity or observes particular taboos. Divinities and ancestors have personalized yearly festivals during which adepts offer sacrificial animals, libations, and favored foods. Such events reinforce the bonds between humanity, ancestors, God, and other deities. They function as modes of communication between humans and spirits. Most significantly, rituals enable supernatural beings to bless individuals and the community with longevity, children, and sustenance. Community rituals may include agricultural rituals designed to persuade the gods to deliver rains and successful harvests and to guarantee healthy livestock. While many rituals involve communal participation, some remain specific to elites whose status, skill, and authority enable them to interact safely and beneficially with sacred powers.

Rites of passage

Rites of passage are rituals marking personal transitions. They coincide with birth and naming, circumcision or coming-of-age initiations, marriage, old age, and death. Each ceremony marks passage from one social status to another. Puberty rites transition a person from childhood to adulthood, when younger members in society learn ancestral knowledge from their elders. The events transpire in seclusion, usually in a natural space (e.g., forests or grasslands) beyond the community's perimeter. Wild areas and natural places—the "bush"—are places where powerful occult forces dwell and can be accessed. This makes them ideal spaces for ceremonies such as initiations, which must at times access dangerous, untamed powers in order to educate children about the world of adulthood. During initiations, same-age youth are gathered together to dwell in this new locale for the duration of their transition. It is a spiritual affair involving prayers and supplications to ancestors, deities, and the Supreme Being for the children's good luck and success.

Tumdo or "male initiation" among the Nandi of Kenya contains several traits common to rites of passage across the continent. Boys belonging to the same age set move away from their parents' homes to dwell in a secluded lodge constructed solely for the ritual's duration. Secret knowledge passes from older men to the boys throughout their time of separation from the community. At the same time, this period serves a practical purpose, preparing boys for adulthood in Nandi society. Tests of bravery and concentration also characterize this initiation. The young boys face challenges, such as having to stare unflinchingly at a grotesque masked figure that threatens them with a spear. The goal is to keep one's eyes on the spearhead without looking away in fear or attuning to the raucous distractions created by the other boys. The spearhead challenge teaches boys to discern immediate priorities from mere distractions. It asks them to develop self-control, and mental and emotional discipline when faced with fear. In other words, manhood requires a mature disposition cultivated by experience. The initiation offers boys preliminary encounters with fear, uncertainty, and psycho-emotional challenges.

Initiated men, warriors, and boys constitute the initiation's primary participants, but women and girls also play significant roles. Mothers, for instance, prepare the meals the boys eat before and after their circumcision ordeal. Mothers also send encouraging gifts throughout the process. Community song-and-dance circles take place four times throughout the initiation process. Women and girls sing encouraging lyrics while boys dance before undergoing their next trial. The boys' female friends sometimes chide them, demanding they prove their bravery if ever they hope to marry. As a rule, initiations are private events, the proceedings are known to only a select few. Nevertheless, the initiates are never entirely beyond the community's reach. Though their passage transpires in the bush, it is the community's prayerful awareness and economic support that insures the ritual's success.

Transition from boyhood to manhood takes a far different form for the Nyae Nyae !Kung in Namibia. Boys undergo ritual scarification after they kill their first male and first female large game. In !Kung belief, elder men in the community prepare traditional medicine powders that bolster one's hunting ability. At a campsite far from the community, the boy receives seven sets of small cuts on his body, each rubbed with a particular medicine. If the game killed is female, he receives cuts on the left side of his body; if it is a male, the cuts are to the right side. This rite qualifies the boy for marriage and cements his status as a hunter. On a social level, the rite means the boy has proven himself able to support a family and to contribute to the community. Whereas the Nandi initiation requires several weeks, the Nyae Nyae !Kung Rite of First Kill takes only a day.

Perhaps the most widely known initiatory societies in Africa are the Poro and Sande societies of West Africa. Poro and Sande are, respectively, the male and female initiatory societies of the Mande and of a number of related peoples who live in Sierra Leone, Liberia, Guinea, and Côte d'Ivoire. At a designated time during puberty, boys and girls are separated by gender and taken by senior society members to live in a specially constructed village in the forest. There, they are initiated into the secrets of the society's gender-specific mysteries. The boys and girls live in the initiatory villages for a year. During this time, they also undergo ritual scarification and circumcision. At the end of the year, they are ready for life as adults, and can now marry and have children.

Initiations for adolescent African girls cause great consternation among Westerners, because they often involve female circumcision. The operation, condemned by the World Health Organization, remains a hotly contested practice around the world. Unfortunately, while Westerners are quick to condemn all such practices and generically lump them under the category of "female genital mutilation," few have much knowledge of what is actually involved. Perhaps most important, female circumcision as practiced in Africa encompasses a wide variety of practices that range dramatically in their extensiveness. Most foreign attention focuses on the most dramatic form of female circumcision, in which the clitoris is fully or mostly removed (clitoridectomy). Medical experts have noted that such a procedure can result in chronic pain, infection, and the loss of the ability to enjoy vaginal intercourse. However, female circumcision in many cultures is considerably less dramatic, involving only partial removal of the clitoris, or only small ritual cuts to the clitoris and labia.

Whether one agrees or disagrees with such circumcision practices, it is worthwhile to point out some reasons to pause before objecting. One especially noteworthy observation is that male circumcision is rarely met with similar opposition. This is in spite of a growing number of Western opponents of male circumcision who argue it is also a form of genital mutilation. They claim it is medically unnecessary and that the foreskin is the male anatomical equivalent of the female clitoris. Nonetheless, because it is culturally "normal" in the West, especially in the United States, its practice in Africa raises few concerns. Likewise, vaginal cosmetic surgery is a growing business in the West. These surgeries often involve removing parts of the vagina, in particular parts of the labia, in order to make it conform to aesthetic standards. Although in many respects these procedures are quite similar to those performed in Africa as female circumcision, they have met with considerably less resistance. While there are many ways in which these surgeries are not entirely parallel to female circumcision, one must nonetheless consider that at least some of the foreign objections to African female circumcision are cultural, rather than strictly humanitarian.

Be that as it may, it is also important to mention not all African female initiations involve circumcision. *Dipo*, an initiatory rite among Krobo women in Ghana, does not. The seminal moment in the ceremony requires girls to sit on a stone made sacred by its connection to Krobo Mountain and the Earth goddess, Nana Kloweki. If the initiand successfully sits down and rises from the stone three times, she passes the purity test. Overall, *dipo* transitions Krobo girls into womanhood by teaching them aesthetics, dance, and household responsibilities. They learn to grind corn, to sweep, and how to wear traditional women's clothing. Until the early nineteenth century, the initiation required the girls' seclusion on Mount Krobo for several months. Economic changes and the adoption of the English academic calendar now cause communities to complete the process within one short week. Nevertheless, the spiritual and social significance remains the same. According to Steegstra, *dipo* serves a pivotal function of purifying girls, thereby making them Krobo women. Ritual cleanliness enables initiates to eat at their neighbor's home and to marry within the community. Krobo diviners conduct ritual cleanings by sprinkling the person's feet with blood from a red hen, symbolically transferring the person's impurity into the animal. Afterward, the diviner slays a white hen and repeats the gestures, thereby removing all misfortune and cleansing her. Preparing girls for womanhood, in this context, involves more than pragmatic instruction. The priestess and the diviner pray over the girls constantly, invoking prosperity, safety, fecundity, peace, and well-being. Steegstra records several moving prayers, which show that idealized Krobo womanhood is about being a successful, contributing member of society who lives peacefully and brings respect to her community. As a rule, such a process always transpires under the gods' auspices. Their appeasement and approval insure *dipo*'s success.

Calendrical rites

Calendrical rites renew the community's connection to the sacred by marking important transitions such as a change between seasons, the first harvest, or planting time. Often, these rites are also believed to renew the world, with the community's ritual actions being a required step in the continued fecundity of the universe. Rainmaking rituals among the Chewa of Mozambique illustrate a seasonal celebration, a calendrical ritual related to important agricultural or pastoral activities. Chewa chiefs burn the bushy Bunda Hill at the end of the rainy season and conform to specific taboos during this event. They pray to *Chiuta*, their Supreme Being and offer snuff at the shrine. If the ritual succeeds, then rain surely follows. A drought, however, suggests that someone violated the taboos and rendered the burning ineffectual.

Chewa priests perform *mfunde*, or "prayers for rain," if a delay in the arrival of storms endangers the farmers' crops. In this instance, community members contribute the maize flour and malt used to prepare the sacrificial meal. However, only children and postmenopausal women may cook the food. Other taboos during this time include a prohibition against conjugal visits. The entire community sleeps outside in order to insure everyone's obedience. In the morning, the priests sacrifice a black goat, and their assistants cook portions of the meat. The ancestors, spirits who negotiate with the Supreme Being on behalf of the living, receive an offering of this meat, alongside maize porridge prepared in the goat broth. It is believed that if these offering and prayers suffice, then the rains will fall.

Annual rain rites among the Ihanzu of Tanzania involve three principal stages. First, the rainmakers (normally a male and female pair) and their assistants perform the *kukumpya lutinde*, or "the cutting-of-the-sod," which involves lighting fire to a *mulama* tree branch. This ritual is a joining of male and female forces, placing the two opposites in balance with one another. The most important event occurs in the shrine. Here, the rainmakers and assistants awake the rainstones by coating them with castor seed oil and sacrificing a black goat. (Like the Chewa, the Ihanzu associate the color black with rain clouds; the goat as well as the rainmakers' ceremonial attire are black.) Following the cutting-of-the-sod, the cohort proceeds to make rain medicine from sacred leaves. They combine the crushed mixture with tepid water and then pour it over the rainstones while praying to the Supreme Being. The water should then begin to boil, without fire. Finally, the rainmaking pair must receive grain tributes gathered from all the villages. The Ihanzu submit the grain to the rainmakers for blessing. After praying over the collected quantities, the powerful pair then mixes and redistributes the grain to each community, returning to them the exact amount they gave. The rains fall shortly after, precipitated by the gender-balanced blessing performed by the rainmakers.

The *buna qalla*, a sacrifice of coffee beans practiced among the Wasa Boorana (part of the Oromo people of East Africa), used to occur several times per month. Recent economic changes, though, have led the community to now conduct this rite only on national holidays. Thus, it has become a commemorative rite. Its ability to reaffirm Boorana cultural identity, in Aguilar's view, still distinguishes it from ceremonies honoring the state's history. Usually, a family invites close friends and neighbors to share in the *buna qalla*. Married women with children fry the coffee beans; only married yet childless women serve them. During this time, men recount cultural history to the children, thus exemplifying how this ritual reinscribes Boorana identity. Once the beans are prepared, a woman prays over them as she places them in the serving dish. Another woman serves the coffee beans by pouring each guest a glass of milk and placing some coffee beans in it. Since the rite represents abundance and prosperity, the guests consume the first glass but leave the second glass half full. They speak blessings to one another while enjoying the beverage. This ritual solidifies the community's dependence on the Supreme Being for blessings, safety, and agricultural prosperity.

Burial rites

Because of a belief in ancestors, funeral rites are especially important to Africans who practice indigious religions. They not only guarantee that the deceased transitions successfully to life as an ancestor, but they also make sure that the new ancestor is pleased with the display of love from his or her family. For this reason, the Ga people of Ghana bury their loved ones in extremely elaborate, customized coffins, which exemplify the deceased's personality and station in life.

Even the announcement of death is often ritualized. When announcing the death of a senior chief in an Òndó-Yorùbá town, the children of the deceased wear their clothes backwards to indicate that it is not a normal time. They proceed to the palace of the king where they announce that their father is gravely ill and is about to join the ancestors. Because it is taboo for the king to take part in burial rituals, all of this must be conveyed through his emissary. The emissary tells the children to go home and take good care of their father. The children then return to the palace to impress on the king the gravity of the illness, and again they are told to do everything humanly possible to make sure their father does not die. On the third and final occasion, they return and announce their father has died. In response, the king's emissaries ritually weep and sing the praises of the deceased chief. After this highly ritualized, prescribed exchange, the death of the high chief will be officially announced to everyone else.

There are several interesting mortuary practices among the Bunyoro of western Uganda. There is an old tradition for the death of a father, the head of the household, in which a small sachet containing millet, simsim (sesame), and fried cow peas is placed in the deceased's hand. The man's children then take and eat small portions of the mixture from the dead man's hand. Beattie learned that this symbolized the deceased's last gesture of care for his children. At the same time, it is interesting to think that this also marks an important role reversal: as an ancestor, the deceased father now depends on his children for food and water.

For the Bunyoro, a father's passing requires his nephew to remove the pole upholding the center of the house. He must also extinguish the fire in the hearth and remove his uncle's bowl from the premises. Then, a fruit-bearing branch from the banana tree must also come down. The nephew scatters all the objects in front of the house. These actions symbolize the destruction of the home. At the same time, one could interpret these actions as physical representations of the father's absence. No longer is he present to uphold the roof over his family's head. His absence means that his eating bowl will always remain empty. Tearing down the fruitful banana branch, like the sachet of grain, suggests that the father is no longer present to provide sustenance for the family. Finally, extinguishing the fire points to his permanent absence. The chaos these broken objects create in the yard indicates a seismic rupture in the family's quotidian life. The family traditionally would not return to this house but would instead construct a new one nearby.

Laying the body to rest also involves protocol specific to the deceased's gender. Males spend their final rest on their right side, while females' bodies lie on the left side. When brushing dirt into the grave, women use their left elbow and men use their right. This gesture signifies that the survivor's hands are useless because she or he may no longer care for the deceased person. Yet one may also interpret this as another indicator that the deceased person's passing has upset the normal order of things. In some sense, burials fracture the social structure, and mortuary rituals signal the community's initial difficulty with adjusting.

A number of African cultures also practice reburial. Reburial is a ritual process in which the remains of a deceased ancestor are exhumed once decomposition is complete and only the bones remain. The bones will frequently then be cleaned, wrapped, and reburied, sometimes in a different location. While reburial practices may sound exotic to many Westerners, they are extremely common throughout the world and are practiced in some European countries, notably Greece. In Madagascar, the island nation off the southeast coast of the African continent, the Malagasy people exhume their ancestors once a decade or so. In preparation for the ritual, called *famadihana*, family tombs will be repaired and restored. On the day of the ritual, the bones of ancestors are removed from the tomb, wrapped in a new white shroud, and then feted with music and dancing. At the end of the party, they are reinterred in the tomb. This ritual continues to be practiced, but in recent years has come under increased opposition from evangelical Christians, who consider it to be an impious and heathen practice.

Marriage rituals

Marriage rituals link two people to one another and to each other's family and community. Many marriage rites across the continent involve a dowry or the exchange of goods between the bride's and groom's families. The rituals involved in Zulu marriages in South Africa include the *lobolo*, a price the groom pays to his bride's family before she marries. Usually eleven cattle comprise the *lobolo* and the husband-to-be makes this payment in several installments. According to Warmelo's investigation, the Zulu believe ancestors bless one with prosperity in the form of cattle. Thus, one could interpret the exchange of cow for bride as a symbol of the new group of ancestors from whom the bride's family now benefits. The recipients acknowledge the gifts by sending beer and firewood prepared by the bride to the future in-law's homestead. Interestingly, all but one animal in the *lobolo* goes to the bride's father. Zulu tradition requires the groom to gift one head of cattle to the bride's mother, payable upon the wedding day. Beyond cattle, the groom must give the *isibizo*, a large monetary sum used to purchase the bride's outfit and to provide other necessary items for the ceremony. Some Zulu fathers charge extraordinary prices, yet the young men are obliged because the nuptials cannot proceed otherwise. Similar to how modern Western brides invite guests to give items listed on the couple's gift registry, Zulu women in the past solicited necessary households items from their neighbors as wedding gifts. The aim was to collect implements the bride would need in her new home. Most importantly, the bride spends several days creating her wedding garments of leather skirts and beaded jewelry, including arm bands, bracelets, and decorative belts.

The actual wedding ceremony lasts four days. Significant moments during the proceedings include the presentation of the *umbeka*, a specially designated animal that represents the bride's ancestors. Both the bride's father and the groom's father say a prayer before exchanging the animal. The bride's father asks the ancestors to acknowledge his daughter in her new state as a married woman. The groom's father asks his ancestors to be at peace with the exchange of cattle for a wife. A similar important occurrence is when the families sacrifice the "wedding ox" to the ancestors. Bathing the bride in the animal's gall associates her with her husband's ancestors, to whose lineage she now belongs. Exchanging cattle for a family's daughter not only compensates for the loss of able-bodied help; it also concretizes a spiritual transaction. Last, divination also informs the wedding ceremony. The new husband must now select one bead concealed in his wife's hands. Ideally he will select the white bead, foretelling a serendipitous union. As in many cultures across the continent, bearing a child cements the marriage.

A number of African marriage rituals include some form of a virginity test for the bride-to-be. During this test, which is frequently symbolic, the groom's family conducts a ritualized examination that is meant to guarantee that the bride is pure.

Ọ̀yọ́-Yorùbá brides in Nigeria wear strands of buttock beads. The virginity test, called *ibálé*, is performed on a bride's wedding night when she arrives at her groom's house. The proof of her virginity is that her buttock beads remain intact. They have not been disturbed by another man, who in a struggle to have sexual contact with her may have broken some of the strands of beads. If the *ibálé* is successful, the groom's parents send gifts, including food and drink, to the bride's parents to thank them for their virtuous safeguarding of the maiden. Among the gifts, they send a full keg of palm wine. However, if the bride fails the *ibálé* test, the groom's parents may send only half a keg, indicating incompleteness, a sign of their displeasure, which may bring shame upon the bride's family and lineage. I should remark that this custom, like several of the ones discussed in this book, has been erased by modernity and changes in African societies.

Rituals and modernity

Xhosa (South Africa) beer-drinking rituals disclose how African rituals have responded to socioeconomic changes among communities. Xhosa customs have long featured home-brewed maize beer. This is, however, a new adaptation of an old practice. Migrant labor among Xhosa men creates patterns of departure and return, events susceptible to witchcraft and misfortune. For this reason, a wife or mother may host an *umsindleko*, a beer-drinking ritual, in honor of the contracted worker. When held before departure, the event solicits the ancestor's protection for the father or husband. The guest of honor gives a few words about why the community has gathered, followed by a reply from one of the guests. The reason for departure is never specifically named, lest one with malevolent intentions should overhear and cause harm to the man. Ideally, the ancestors will hear the group's words and protect the man on his journey.

An *umsindleko* may also be held upon the man's return, yet this ritual remains infrequent. Many households host this event only once every five years in the man's career. When held upon his return, the *umsindleko* marks either the man's economic success or his inability to earn enough money for his family. In either case, the ritual implores the ancestors to help the man profit from his next venture to the mines. Invited guests seat themselves according to gender and age. The first round of beer, called *iimvuko* or "awakening," is dedicated to the host group. It identifies and sets apart the first group present at the event. Several smaller, formalized servings follow. These drinks mark the liaisons in the group, those who represent the groups before the chiefs. These liaisons receive pitchers of beer and then share them among their separate groups. The *intselo* or "main drink," may be dispersed according to number (if only a few people attend) or via social groups. Several customary principles organize this event, including the rule that women receive less beer than men and their glasses are the last ones filled. In similar fashion, the younger people receive beer after the older attendees. Importantly, reciprocity determines how much beer each group receives. Those who gave generously when hosting their own beer drinks receive plenty at the current gathering. *Ukuqwela*, "emptying the pot," concludes the event and is signaled by the host group serving the last pitcher of beer to its members and the elders of the invited cohorts. Customarily, the last glass returns to the eldest man in the host group, who then consumes it and announces when it is finished. The beer drink is a ritual seeking ancestral blessings for the migrant worker. At the same time, this rite reestablishes the man's obligations to his community. It celebrates his return to his family and admonishes him to avoid a morally lax lifestyle in urban South African cities.

Festivals

African traditional religions usually feature festivals honoring divinities or cultural heroes. The Òṣun festival held annually in Òṣogbo, Nigeria, lasts sixteen days and has become a popular transnational event. The *Àtaója*, the *ọba* (king) of Òṣogbo, invites a babaláwo to consult the sacred oracle, Ifá, and inquire about when the celebration should begin. Once the opportune date becomes apparent, the *Àtaója* travels in a royal procession to the market where he announces the forthcoming date and names the sacrificial items required. A few days after this proclamation, the *olójúmérìndínlógún*, or "lighting of the sixteen candles" in the *Àtaója*'s palace, marks the festival's official beginning. This moment involves lighting local cotton soaked in palm oil. These flames rest on sixteen trays extending like branches from a brass pillar and are burned from mid-evening until dawn.

Finally, the main event in the Òṣun festival is when the major Òṣun priestesses process deep into the Òṣun Grove to the Òṣun River and perform sacrificial rites to the goddess within her temple. Other adepts dance and sing outside the temple while the community awaits word of the offering's success. Eventually, the priestesses emerge and perform another ritual at the riverbank. This moment consecrates the river and signals when community members may bathe in the blessed waters. Diedre Bádéjo notes, in particular, that participants include women who collect the water for spiritual medicinal uses throughout the year and women who are seeking to bear children. Òṣun is the Yorùbá goddess of fertility, and her annual festival celebrates the births she has brought into the community. It also provides an auspicious moment to pray for barren women.

Considered a cultural hero rather than a god, Olófin in Ìdànrè, Nigeria, is a brother of Odùduwà, the cultural hero who founded the Yorùbá sacred city of Ilé-Ifè in Nigeria and became the first king there. Olófin receives tribute during the Iden festival. The festival coincides with the year's end, a time at which the deceased are counseled for guidance. During this event, the Owá, ruler of Idanre, represents Olófin on Earth. Olófin, according to oral history, parted ways with Odùduwà's followers after his brother's demise. Olófin performed various rituals, such as chalking the Owá's body to resemble Olófin and initiating the festival by first

69

4. The Maundy Thursday foot-washing ceremony at the Church of
St. John Evangelist in Addis Ababa, Ethiopia, 1974.

honoring the Ọwá's ancestors. Another interesting ritual is the repeated washing of the Ọwá's feet during his procession to Iden Hill. Several attendants wash the ruler's feet with spiritual herbal medicines designed to erase his footsteps so that malevolent people may not follow him. Importantly, the Ọwá carries royal vestitures from Ọlófin's early days in the palace at Ilé-Ifẹ̀. His same crown, scepter, and velveteen cloth adorn the Ọwá in the present-day Iden festival. The event reaches its height when the Ọwá dances on the Iden and replaces the crown on his head with the same spiritual medicine used to protect the precious emblem for centuries. There is an emphasis on personal and communal ancestors. During the festival's peak, the Ọwá thanks the crown for enduring all these years. In some sense, the Ọwá gives thanks to the persons and powers responsible for his kingdom's longevity. Similarly, dedicating the Iden festival to Ọlófin is ancestral veneration quintessentially large.

Festivals not only renew the bonds between ancestors and their progeny but also emphasize cyclical time as well as keeping track of the community's legacy and orientation by carrying forward its predecessors' memories.

Chapter 5
Sacred arts and ritual performances

As there is no strict separation between the sacred and secular in traditional African cultures, it follows that arts and material culture are influenced by religious practice and traditions. Using the word "art" in an African context can have confusing and unintended consequences. In the West, art is now often understood to exist for its own sake. This is a departure from the standard prior to the twentieth century, in which art typically had religious and specifically devotional aims. With the secularization of public life in the West, art increasingly took on a secular quality.

Although decorative and folk arts have continued to be cultivated in the West, they have often been seen as inferior to the "high" arts. When displayed in Western museums, African sacred objects tend to be classified as examples of folk or "primitive" art, or as decorative ornamentation for common-use objects. Viewed in museums, where they often are stripped of their cultural and religious contexts, these objects are portrayed to audiences as examples of African art objects. This has the unfortunate consequence of creating an artificial environment in which these objects—such as masks and statues portraying spirits—are viewed in a fashion entirely unrelated to the ways they were seen by their makers and intended viewers.

Museums typically encourage viewers to see art objects as static, when in fact many African art objects are designed to be interactive and serve integral functions in religious practices. Many of the statues, sculptures, staffs, crowns, and masquerades are often tangible representations of the gods, ancestors, or divine entities, or else are made to honor or invoke them. These objects often also serve as protective talismans. However, it seems important not to abandon the term "art" outright as a way of describing such objects, lest the mistake be made of assuming that they are therefore aesthetically and technically inferior to their Western counterparts that earn the label.

African art scholars have highlighted the difficulties that have attended the study of African arts, due in large part to the Western lens through which they have been conventionally analyzed. These scholars point out the fallacies and weaknesses inherent in this approach, which has often sought to make broad generalizations about African art without really understanding the culture and society in which an object was produced. Without understanding Zulu cosmology and the significance of colors and patterns within their culture, it would be difficult to properly understand the meanings of the intricate beading patterns the Zulu use to communicate their perceptions of their lives. Much of African art is made for spiritual and ritual use, and the variant different forms that this art takes points to the breadth, diversity, and innovativeness in African material and religious culture.

African material culture is rich and diverse, ranging from ancient rock art to the sophisticated bronze statues and monumental bas-relief panels of Dahomey. The majesty, naturalism, and scale of these arts have often so impressed the Europeans who "discovered" them that they sometimes attributed their creation to earlier Indo-Europeans who had trekked through Africa. More ludicrously, the German explorer Leo Frobenius believed that bronzes he "found" in Togo and Nigeria were of such technical and artistic merit that they were evidence of the lost civilization

5. The Zanbeto masquerade in Ouidah, Benin, is associated with the secret society of the Fon people. The performer's regalia, covered in brightly colored straw, is believed to provide protection against the evil eye and malevolent spirits.

of Atlantis. On January 30, 1911, the *New York Times* reported that Frobenius had discovered in Togo a bronze bust of Poseidon that could not possibly have been made by Africans. He believed that it was evidence that Atlantis had not only been real but that it had been located in western Africa. The blatant racism of these European explorers inhibited their ability to conceive of the fact that Africans had created these sculptures and built magnificent city structures. Unfortunately, this mindset still persists in African art history today.

The most common and well-known kinds of African arts are statuettes, figurines, and vessels. The multiple uses to which these figurines are put include representations of ancestors and storage containers for traditional medicines. Sometimes, these are used as vessels to spiritually enhance medicines, or as containers for the magical ingredients that empower a spiritual entity. The *boli* sculptures of the Bamana, made from clay, fabric, and other ingredients, are molded around a pouch of herbs that is said to "control the uncontrollable desires of men." Among the Ga'anda of northern Nigeria, the ceramic vessels become the way in which the recently deceased maintain a tangible, though temporary, presence among the living. The Senufo of northern Côte d'Ivoire, Mali, and Burkina Faso design caryatid drums featuring women in both a seated position and a load-bearing position, which praises women's industriousness, vigor, and invaluable maternal role. The Tabwa of the Democratic Republic of Congo and Zambia use carved wooden figurines not only to represent ancestral figures but also to protect and heal individuals during bouts of sickness. As one can see, these objects are made a variety of ways, and their uses encompass a broad range of spiritual functions.

Although critics decry the fact that many statues are erroneously taken to be ancestral in nature, within many African cultures small statuettes are used as representations of the ancestors or recently deceased family members. These statues are often thought of as more than simple representations. In many instances, they are tangible icons used to communicate with the ancestor, insuring the ancestor's presence in the quotidian lives of the living. Statuettes for a deceased twin, *ìbejì*, are common among the Yorùbá. The Tabwa of Tanzania also use figurines called *mpundu* to represent a twin who has died young. The mother carries the wooden figure until the surviving twin can walk. The Fang of southern Cameroon and Gabon employ wooden statues as reliquary guards; these are perched on the edge of the bark containers in which the skull of an ancestor is kept. Among the Akan of Ghana and the Anyi of Côte d'Ivoire, terracotta heads are adorned and dressed in rich fabrics and metals to prepare the recently deceased for his or her journey to the place of the ancestors. Whether used for communication or commemoration, these ancestral icons comprise a large part of the material culture of African traditional religious practices.

Surely some of the most visually striking and well-known African statutes are the *minkisi* (singular *nkisi*) from west-central Africa. These wooden anthropomorphic statues often include mirrors and have nails driven into them. Because of the nails, they have an arresting and somewhat grotesque quality that makes them appealing as showpieces in museums and galleries. It is a mistake, though, to assume that the presence of nails indicates that the figure is tormented. On the contrary, the nails usually represent points of power. *Minkisi* typically have plant medicines and mystical objects inside of them whose properties indicate the characteristics belonging to the spirit embodied by the figurine. Often, these medicines are embedded behind the mirror that the figure holds in its belly. The mirror also enables it to deflect evil. For each request or supplication that is made of the *nkisi*, a nail will be driven into it. A powerful *nkisi* will also sometimes be used as a witness to an oath-swearing or pact between two individuals. In this case, a nail will be driven into the *nkisi* to show that the spirit will guarantee that both parties honor their vows. As living, ensouled beings, *minkisi* obviously pose ethical challenges when displayed in museum collections. In some cases, the medicines are removed, at which time the figure becomes simply a statue. Unfortunately, this is not always the case, and then the museum is in fact displaying a living being—a person, basically—without providing for the adequate care and respect of that being.

6. A *nkisi* figure from the Congo in central Africa, ca. 1880–1920. The carved wooden nail-studded sculpture has a mirrored container for keeping potent medicine.

Art in religious celebration

Festivals comprise a huge part of religious practice in Africa. The celebratory nature of this aspect of religious worship is usually enhanced by the presence of masquerade performances. As with the statues and figurines, these masquerades represent a host of spiritual entities, including ancestors, gods, and animal tutelaries. Masquerades among the Efik of southern Nigeria portray the leopard, a major tutelary spirit. In Tanzania, the Tabwa still use a buffalo mask during masquerades, speculated to represent masculine aggressive energy. These masquerades range from simple wooden carved masks to elaborate outfits made of animal skin, cloth, shells, leaves, beads, fur, and feathers. Some masks are recognizably human or animal, while others are unrecognizable as any terrestrial entity. One of the ancestral masquerades among the Yorùbá, called *egúngún*, sometimes resembles a pile of hay, the costume being constructed from shredded palm fronds, called *màrìwò*. The Chewa of eastern Zambia, one of the few east African cultures to continue with a masquerade tradition, have a masquerade called *Nyau*, which is used to transport the newly deceased out of the land of the living to the spiritual realm. The *nyau* mask is made entirely of basketry and is set on fire once it has enticed the spirit out of the house and into the forest.

The Hemba, who live in the Democratic Republic of Congo along the shores of Lake Tanganyika, are known for a unique mask called *mwisi wa so'o*. Although reminiscent of a were-chimpanzee with a grotesquely wide mouth, it is neither human nor animal and is believed to occupy the same liminal space as a recently departed soul. The masquerade is seen during funerals, when it chases women and children into their homes. Its unbounded wildness does not respect normal social boundaries until it is forced to do so in the latter part of the funeral ceremonies.

Among some cultures like the Salampasu of the Congo, a masquerade is danced during the circumcision initiation ceremony.

In Burkina Faso, the Bwa are noted for their particularly impressive masks. One mask representative of a serpent can extend up to six or seven feet into the air. These elaborately carved animal-inspired masks, including the butterfly and the snake, are thought to bring fertility to the crops. They also assist in maintaining balance between the settled community and the supernatural forces inhabiting the surrounding untamed bush. These masks are mostly painted black, white, and red in geometric designs. The Guro elite of Côte d'Ivoire, also seeking to maintain the balance with their natural environment, cultivate a sacred relationship with forest creatures who are propitiated in a ceremonial masquerade. While one of the three masquerades, Gu, represents a female entity, women are not allowed to dance the masquerade. They are, nonetheless, "mother[s] of the mask," and an elder female is charged with the ritual feeding of the mask. The mask is taken to the girl's circumcision ceremony and small drops of blood are dropped on the mask to charge and feed its essence. The mask is then returned to its male keepers. While many African masquerades do not permit the participation or presence of women, women in some cases are keepers of the masquerade, as with the Kono of Liberia.

One of the most studied African masquerades is the Gèlèdé festival of the Yorùbá of Nigeria. While the Gèlèdé festival celebrates the power of women, women are forbidden from participating in the masquerading itself. Instead, the masquerade is danced by men, who don wooden masks that portray female spirits and dress in costumes that comically portray accentuated breasts and hips (see illustration 1, p. 25). The Gèlèdé performance is said to promote social harmony, fertility, and survival. It is also a reminder to the community of the feminine force and its necessity to the community's continued prosperity and progress.

The women of the Sande secret societies of the Mende people appear to be some of the only females who actually wear masks and dance in a masquerade. Newly initiated into the women's

Sande society, girls return to the village as Mende women wearing Sowei masks. The mask is said to represent the moral, spiritual, and aesthetic ideals of the Sande society and female beauty, which includes artfully arranged and elaborate hairstyles, an expression of inner calmness, and a small mouth and small ears. The diminutive size of the mouth and ears are to indicate that the ideal woman is not a gossip and does not listen to words of seduction. If an animal adorns the top of the mask, it is said to attest to the dancer's quality as well as to indicate the connection between this world and that of the ancestors and the gods. But there are masks that are not created to be worn. Among the Mano of Liberia, a blacksmith traditionally was given the position of judge. He used the mask by placing it on the floor and presenting the case to it, then interpreted the mask's response. The bottom of the mask has what appears to be twine with a rock attached to the end of it. These were to indicate the number of people "killed by the mask's supernatural power or executed in its name". The Mano also had a hornbill mask that was used to supernaturally judge disputes between families, the collection of debts, or even something as apparently mundane as supervising food distribution at a funeral.

A few words need to be said about some common misconceptions that outsiders have about African masquerading festivals. First of all, outsiders often assume that the masks themselves are of enormous antiquity, or that the oldest masks would be the most prized. In fact, many African masquerading traditions make new masks every time the masquerade is performed. Old masks are often destroyed or discarded. In such cases, the tradition is in the performance of the masquerade, not in the masks themselves. Often a balance is struck between old masks and new masks. The most sacred masks of the Sande societies are quite old and are believed to have been carved by water spirits. These masks can be danced only by senior initiates of the society. New masks are being created all the time and are also danced in the masquerade. Second, it is often wrongly assumed that the themes portrayed in masquerades are from time immemorial. In fact, masquerades are constantly incorporating new, relevant themes. African masquerades frequently incorporate masks that represent colonists and foreigners. As such, masquerading traditions are not relics of the past, but up-to-date and timely reflections of the lives of their performers and audiences.

Beadwork

Intricate and elaborate beadwork is a hallmark of material culture in many African communities. While beadwork dates back to ancient times in Africa, the arrival of glass beads with European contact had a profound effect on this form of African material culture. The significance of the beads often lies in the patterns and the colors. Certain colors are sacred to certain supernatural entities or forces and thus, when worn by an individual, invoke the protection of those forces.

Chief among beading traditions in southern Africa are those of the Zulu and Xhosa, in which beads are used to create necklaces, earrings, and bracelets that protect the wearer from malevolent supernatural forces. These groups are renowned for the striking geometrical patterns and pairing of bold colors in their beadwork. The Zulu and Xhosa also use beads to adorn skirts, shirts, vests, and aprons with complex designs in order to communicate the wearer's marital status, social rank, or spiritual state. These beads are thus a primary means by which these South African groups express their spiritual, social, and economic lives.

In West Africa, the Yorùbá have also mastered this skill. The Yorùbá make entire sacred objects out of delicate, and often expensive, beads. The *adé* (crown) of the Yorùbá kings are magnificent beaded works of art that are said to not only contain the mystical powers of sacred entities but also to transmit this sacred power to the king (see illustration 2 on p. 41). The power of the crown is reinforced by the intricate arrangement of birds on top that are said to signify the female power of mothers and witches.

The curtain of beads that hides the king's face provides a barrier between the power of the king's gaze and the public. It also serves as a reminder to the public that the king is not an ordinary person but someone who possesses supernatural power and divine status.

The Bamum of the Cameroon grasslands decorate carved wooden statues, thrones, and footstools with beads. The beads are used to indicate the prestige and divine status of the objects they cover. This applies particularly to the throne and footstool of the king of the Bamum. Before presenting the stool to the king, a high priest will smear the stool's underside with sacrificial blood and nestle spiritual medicines inside it. This ritual infuses the throne with divine power, which dissipates upon the king's death, at which time the throne will be buried with the king.

The Kuba and their neighbors the Luba are two communities in central Africa known for their elaborate beadwork, which adorns their kings' regalia and the sacred instruments used in ceremonies. The outfits the kings wear are made up of numerous pieces, including a beaded tunic, arm and leg protectors, and a heavy helmet-like crown. The Luba's divinatory priests wear intricately beaded headdresses and a plethora of beaded necklaces when they are possessed.

Orality and music: performance in African religions

African traditional cultures are largely oral in nature. Knowledge about the ancestors, the deities, clan history, and local politics is transmitted through storytelling, songs, praise poetry, and face-to-face conversations. It would be a mistake to assume, because of this, that Africa does not have a rich and extensive history of written culture. Egyptian hieroglyphics is one of the oldest written languages. The high Christian civilization of Ethiopia created an enormous body of literature in *Ge'ez* and preserved a number of important Christian documents in translation. Likewise, the

Muslim civilization of northern Africa had not only a large body of original literature in Arabic—especially medical and scientific texts—but also preserved a tremendous number of antique texts, which they reintroduced to medieval Europe through Spain. Everywhere that Islam was introduced to Africa, written Arabic followed. One of the largest universities of the medieval world was located in Timbuktu, in the empire of Mali. It is believed that the libraries of the university likely held more than a million volumes in Arabic. Therefore, the cultural and religious emphasis in much of Africa on orality over the written word must be viewed as the result more of preference than necessity.

The significance of orality and speech in Africa can be seen in the many words that diverse cultural groups use to describe a wise or intelligent person. For the Limba and the Barundi, a person is clever if he or she uses speech well. Most African societies praise singers who recite not only a person's lineage but also the achievements of that lineage or clan. Words hold power. This performative aspect of African societies becomes even more pronounced in religious practice. Epic tales, songs for the deities, praise poetry, incantations, and recitation of divination verses are all examples of this rich verbal art. According to the Dinka of Sudan, "a person's creative speech is . . . an integral part of his ethos or personality." Words have the power to bring things into being and imbue them with life.

During religious ceremonies, music is almost always present. Music in these instances is a language that speaks to the deities and sacred beings. The chanting of priests and the musical accompaniment, usually played on drums, communicate in a mystical language that the deities understand and to which they feel compelled to respond. In the sacred festival for Odùduwà, the first king and ancestor of the Yorùbá people, a sacred percussive instrument, called ęgańrań, is used, since drumming is prohibited. Ęgańrań is a set of iron gongs that produce percussive, exhilarating rhythmic sounds when beaten together. The voice of

the priest or priestess has been endowed with mystical power, due
to the exalted spiritual status he or she achieves during initiation.
There is also usually training and apprenticeship involved in
learning how to turn the voice into an instrument to engage
supernatural forces. It is not necessarily every priest or priestess
who will have the voice necessary to sing and call the deities to
inhabit human vessels during possession. The ìjálá chanters of the
Yorùbá are believed to be divinely inspired by the deity Ògún.

Epic tales such as the Mwindo epic of the Banyanga (Democratic
Republic of Congo) or the Malian Sundiata epic tell of man's heroic
adventures, battles, and triumphs with and over the deities. These
epics are significant, because they reinforce the reciprocity of the
relationship between humans and their deities. Some African
groups, like the Lega and Mongo peoples of central Africa, even
believe that bards receive their ability and knowledge about how to
perform their tales from divine inspiration.

Diviners' speech, by virtue of the powers given to them during their
initiation, has the ability to invoke powerful supernatural entities.
For the Ifá priests of the Yorùbá, the reciting of divinatory verse is
a powerful act that may at times induce the desired results for their
clients without any further action being required. African peoples
have long believed that sounds and words can also have strong
negative effects. This is demonstrated by the statues of sacrificial
victims that have been unearthed in Ilé-Ifè, Nigeria, and which
are thought to have had their mouths bound so as not to be able to
place curses upon their executioners. Witches are also known for
the power their words possess. They are especially feared for their
abilities to curse those who have incurred their wrath.

Divinatory art

Divination is an integral part of African religious practice. Many of
these divination practices use objects specifically made and ritually
enhanced for the purpose of divination. The sacred objects used

for divination include wooden statues, animal bones, intricately designed gourds, and beautifully beaded pouches. The Luba Bilumbu diviners of the Democratic Republic of Congo use highly decorated and sculpted gourds believed to contain the proofs and promises of their profession. They consult the microcosm of spirits that inhabit the gourd to sort out the problems of their clients. Sometimes, these gourds contain sculpted figures that represent the spirits present in the gourd. The Guro of Côte d'Ivoire are well known for their unique mouse divination practices. Reading the tracks and movements of the mouse through a series of sacred bones, the diviner is able to divine the problems of their clients. The diviners also keep by their beds two carved figures, often a male and female, to offer protection against and repel illness. These carved figures are ritually offered food, money, and other valuable items. They also serve as messengers from the spirit world who inform the diviner where to find herbs to remedy his clients' problems. The implements of the Yorùbá babaláwo include an elaborately carved tray that usually features the face of the messenger god Èṣù on the top. Babaláwo also carry an elaborately carved ritual tapper that is used to mark time during the recitation of divination poetry. The diviner's pouch for his instruments is usually an intricately designed beaded bag. Often, diviners will also have a mounted carved bowl for the sixteen sacred palm nuts used in divination. The bowl frequently depicts scenes that represent the continuity of life or a figure representing the search for knowledge or wisdom.

Body art and style

For many African societies, art is not simply about material culture and tangible objects. The body becomes a natural canvas to honor the deities and to seek their protection and beauty. Although many of the bodily beautification practices serve to identify clan, lineage, and social hierarchies, there are instances in which these practices are employed for spiritual purposes. Vodun initiates in West Africa often wear hairstyles that are indicative of the god to whom they are dedicated. Because the god is seen as residing in the head of the initiate, this focus on the care of the head is fitting and also serves the purpose of making initiates instantly recognizable to those familiar with the tradition. Likewise, many initiates of West African religious traditions have their heads shaved during the course of the initiation.

Body painting is also common during initiations, with circles, lines, and spots being made with vegetable and mineral paints to indiciate the power of the spirits. Ritual cuts are also often made in the skin of the head, face, arms, torso, and legs during this time. These cuts are used as a way to introduce medicines into the body of the initiate but, again, also serve as decorative body modifications, which make the initiate recognizable for those who can "read" such marks. The Oromo of Ethiopia cover their bodies with raised scars that are rubbed with medicines to protect the wearer and ward off bad spirits. In Mozambique, the Makonde found that raised body tattoos were so significant that they featured them in many of their carved wooden figures. Sometimes, what makes these body markings sacred has more to do with the implements used to make them than with the markings themselves. Among the Yorùbá, the iron tools of the òrìṣà Ògún are used in this process, and thus demonstrate the transformative power of the deity: what was plain becomes more beautiful and is spiritually protected or enhanced.

The intersection between Mende female beauty standards and religious ideals can be seen in Sande initiation rites, which teach girls certain standards of beauty and comportment. Often, these religious standards taught by the secret societies are difficult to distinguish from nonreligious Mende notions of beauty. The mermaid deity Tingoi is the ultimate embodiment of Mende ideas of female beauty. Like the sacred masks of the Sande society, Tingoi has small facial features, a fair complexion, long black hair, and a long lined neck. Very beautiful women are sometimes compared to her. Another aesthetic ideal is that of the *haenjo*, the pubescent girl on the day when she emerges from her Sande initiation as a newly made Mende woman. To live up to this beauty standard, her complexion must be beautiful and clear, her eyes clear and courteous, she must be well dressed, and her hair must be perfectly styled. Hair style is one of the most important aspects of Mende womanhood. Women are supposed to have long, black, well-oiled, and full-bodied hair. New initiates have their hair pulled up and piled on top of their heads in a knot, a style that mimics sacred Sande masks and is seen as the height of female beauty. Mende women keep their hair tightly braided so that the shape of the head is clearly visible, since the round shape of the head is considered extremely beautiful. They also go out of their way to have unique, elaborate braids, which they keep tight and well groomed. This is considered one of the most important signs of beauty and is particularly important as a way for a woman to show her commitment to her husband's pleasure. Although some of these aesthetic ideals are technically secular, these discussions show how much secular beauty ideals are embedded in and influenced by Sande traditions.

Clothing is often also dictated in part by religious concerns. The initiation societies we have discussed all have specific outfits that initiates wear at various stages during the process. The importance of bridal clothing has also been mentioned. Many initiatory societies also dictate styles and colors of clothing that can be worn by initiates. For example, initiates of Ifá in Nigeria are usually required to wear only white for at least a year after initiation, and sometimes for much longer. The kente cloth of the Asante people of Ghana is world famous for its bright colors and intricate geometric designs. This cloth, made by hereditary craftsmen, is often given as a gift for religious occasions, such as birth, naming, and marriage celebrations. The colors and patterns of the cloth all convey meaning, and the cloth is chosen to correspond to specific events. It is intended to be worn only for special occasions, often those of a ceremonial or religious nature. Certain patterns are worn only by people of high stature, such as chiefs and kings. The way that the cloth is worn has symbolic significance. Kings and people of high stature—as well as those celebrating extremely special occasions—will wear the kente so that it drags on the ground. This signifies their lives are bountiful enough that they can afford to damage the expensive cloth, because they can replace it.

African visual and oral life are textured with religious meaning. In the contemporary period, African art objects are interpreted in the context of African's historical and cultural experiences. Even bodily comportment, dress, and grooming are influenced by religious ideals. In order to understand the true scope and significance of African art, it is necessary to understand how deeply influenced it is by religious conventions and meaning.

Chapter 6
Christianity and Islam in Africa

Africa domesticated the two exogenous religions. While Islam and Christianity both came to Africa from outside, both traditions have been present on the African continent for nearly as long as they have existed. This means that Africans have had centuries to develop unique adaptations to Christian and Islamic practices, and theologies to make them well suited to African needs. It also means that in many respects neither can be considered particularly foreign to Africa; in some cases, their African forms are older than certain "traditional religions." In the same way that Islam and Christianity have changed, so too have traditional religions, which in some cases have adopted entirely new forms. This is an important corrective to the tendency to view traditional religions as old and global religions as new. In fact, all religions are always changing and incorporate both old and new aspects into their practices.

First contact

Christianity appeared on the African continent very early in its history. In particular, north Africa hosted an efflorescence of Christianity that was instrumental in shaping the early Church. Africa is mentioned in the biblical narrative a number of times: as a baby, Jesus was taken to Egypt for protection; one of the most significant episodes in the book of Acts recounts the baptism of an Ethiopian eunuch by Philip the Evangelist (Acts 8); Saint Augustine, one of Christianity's most important theologians, was Bishop of Hippo (present-day Algeria); and the Christian writer Tertulian was from Carthage (present-day Tunisia). Notably, both Augustine and Tertulian were Latin speakers and lived in Roman provinces of Africa, which recalls the extent to which Africa was integral to the classical world.

Christianity entered the African continent via the Roman Empire in north Africa. When Rome converted to Christianity, so too did its colonies. For this reason, Christianity took hold in Egypt. However, the heresy of Monophysitism separated the Egyptian church from the majority of Christendom, which adopted the Chalcedonian position that Christ was both entirely human and entirely divine or had two natures. Monophysites believe that Jesus had only a divine nature, rather than being both human and divine. This belief defined the early Egyptian Coptic Church, which was the first form of institutional Christianity organized on the African continent. It was also here that the first Christian monastic tradition began among what was subsequently called the "Desert Fathers." From Egypt, the religion spread to Nubia. Missionary involvement in the sixth century helped convert more people throughout the kingdom to the Coptic Church. Over time, indigenous religious and ritual practices changed. For example, Nubian rulers ceased building tombs and pyramids. Indigenous sacred kingship required food, servants, and weapons to accompany the mummified king into the afterlife, but upon converting to Christianity, deceased leaders were merely wrapped in cloth and laid facing east so that they might see Jesus, when he returned like the rising sun. The greatest shift manifested in new churches, which were built in numerous Nubian towns, was the bringing of liturgy into the people's quotidian lives. Previously, the emphasis on sacred kingship seemed to limit Christian religious practice to elite political leaders.

North African Christianity's golden age did not last long, though. In the seventh century, Islam established itself on the Arabian Peninsula, and restless Arab soldiers were expanding by the eighth century into north Africa. A century-long *jihad* waged by Arabs in Egypt converted the country from Christianity to Islam. Egyptian Christians welcomed the new establishment, because they had suffered under Byzantine rule. The conversion occurred, at least in part, due to economic pressure: the Arabs demanded conversion or payment of *jizya* (tax on non-Muslims), for which all Jews and Christians remained accountable. The conversion to Islam freed Egyptians from a heavy financial burden, while also releasing them from theological tensions with Rome. Nubia resisted conversion by signing a nonaggression pact with the Arab government, in which they agreed to provide desirable goods to Egypt each year. Nevertheless, Nubian Christianity gave way to Islam in 1272 when its regent submitted to Arab rulers from Egypt. Abdallah Barshambo became the first outwardly Muslim Nubian king in 1315. At the same time, Islam was actively converting the Berbers, who were the indigenous people in the Maghreb (meaning west in Arabic, this area encompasses Morocco, Algeria, Tunisia, Libya, and Mauritania). Although the Berbers were at first resistant, they eventually converted and from them emerged a number of fundamentalist groups, notably the Almoravids, which actively sought to expand the territory of Islam.

Christianity entered Aksum, in modern-day Ethiopia, in the third century. Frumentius and Aedesius, two Christians, befriended King Ella Amida of Aksum. They eventually mentored the king's son, Ezana. Ezana became a Christian, and once Frumentius became a bishop, he welcomed Frumentius openly into his kingdom. Upon becoming king, Ezana along with Abuna Salama worked to evangelize Ethiopia. He succeeded, and Christianity became the dominant religion by his reign's end. In the fifth century, nine monks from Syria introduced monasticism to the region and founded Debre Damo, a cliff monastery in Tigre province.

Further developments

The Ibadites, who differ from Sunni and Shi'ite Muslims because of their belief that the Qu'ran is created rather than the uncreated word of God, were the first to introduce Islam to West Africa. Islam arrived in tandem with commercial trade, thereby presenting its language and culture as a useful lingua franca among merchants from diverse ethnic groups. Islam provided a distinct moral code that facilitated trade between groups. Yet its influence on indigenous kingdoms grew slowly. In ancient Ghana, Muslim merchants resided in separate enclaves rather than among the general population. There, they constructed mosques and instituted their own political structures. War Dyabi of Takrur, in modern-day Senegal, was the first West African leader to convert to Islam. This marked an early trend of political leaders converting while their subjects remained loyal to their indigenous beliefs.

This pattern changed in the eleventh century when several chiefs and kings along critical trade routes also converted to Islam, thus normalizing the religion's presence in sub-Saharan communities. During this period, the Sudanese empire grew and expanded; West African Islam experienced a golden age, during which Islam flowered in great cities like Timbuktu, Gao, Jenne, and Dia. In these places, Islamic sciences, culture, and arts were firmly established. A historic conversion occurred in the thirteenth century when Sundiata, king of Mali, became a Muslim. Sundiata's equally famous descendant, Mansa Musa, created numerous mosques and Islamic educational institutions throughout the expanding empire. Mansa Musa's *hajj* to Medina and Mecca has become fabled as a testament to the great wealth of the Malian empire. During the trip, everywhere he stopped on a Friday, he ordered a mosque to be built. He spent so much that the price of gold temporarily fell when he passed through Egypt. However, Islam's prominence among political leaders meant that it began to recede once the Malian empire fell. From the ashes of Ancient Mali grew another famous Sudanese empire, Songhai, who like Mali boasted of powerful rulers such as Sunni Ali and Askia the Great. While kings, chiefs, merchants, and clerics in the western Sudanese empires became Muslims, most of the general population remained loyal to indigenous beliefs. Thus, it became possible for Bambara religious praxis to endure the Muslim tide in what is now the Mali nation state. Nonetheless, many in this region remain Muslim to this day, in part owing to the conversions of these great leaders.

Islamicization of East Africa followed trade routes through Ethiopia, a primarily Christian kingdom. The fall of Christian Egypt and Nubia facilitated Islam's acceptance along the horn of Africa and central-eastern coastal regions. Muslim traders from Oman and the Middle East sought to establish Indian Ocean links through trade routes with Kenya and Tanzania, and in the process, Islam was also introduced to those areas. The Somali maintained their cultural identity while converting to Islam because the Muslim immigrants arrived in smaller numbers; rather than a total Arabization of the region, Somali culture absorbed the clusters of merchants and clerics who entered the region. Consequently, the Somali kingdom successfully upheld its distinct cultural practices.

In time, Arabic-speaking Muslims began to penetrate inland and encountered Bantu speakers. This led to the emergence of Kiswahili language and culture, the most popular African language today, and with it the further spread of Islam in eastern Africa. With the establishment of trans-Saharan trade routes, the slave trade developed. Black Africans, primarily from western Africa, were taken north to the Maghreb, as well as east to the Indian Ocean. This trade resulted in a sizable number of black slaves being sent to Morocco, Libya, and Algeria, where one continues to find their descendents. Black slaves were also sent to the Middle East, including Saudi Arabia and Kuwait. Additionally, a small but appreciable number of black Africans were sold as slaves in south Asia by way of the Indian Ocean.

Africa was no tabula rasa when Abrahamic religions arrived on the continent. Consequently, indigenous cultures impacted Islamic and Christian practice just as much as these traditions left impressions upon their new milieu. The chief of the Barghawata, who lived in what is now Morocco, developed a new religion by scripting a Qur'an in Berber. Salih ibn Tarif also developed new ways of worship, pulling from both Islamic and indigenous rituals. Importantly, he deemed himself a prophet, the logical spearhead for this new religion. This was perhaps the most robust example of an indigenized Islamicism in North Africa.

Islam underwent other long-lasting Africanizations, most apparent in the amulets worn by contemporary adherents. These protective adornments consisted of both a written and a graphic component. The written part may be a Qur'an verse or passages from Islamic divination manuals and books on numerology. Usually, the diviner scripts the text in Arabic. The visual component may include magic squares or planetary references. Such creations are acceptible in African Islam because it is Allah, his angels, and the good *djinn* who empower it. This practice combines the creation of amulets, an indigenous African praxis, with a deep faith in the Qur'an and its power. In this way, African spiritual practice has refashioned Islamic tradition.

The second phase of African Christianity resulted from Iberian Portuguese contact with west and west-central Africa through the process of maritime exploration. The Roman Catholic Church supported the Portuguese Crown's trade activities on the African continent, with the rationale that it provided an opportunity to spread the Christian message to previously unevangelized areas. While the Portuguese did make some contact with the kingdoms of West Africa such as the Benin and Warri Kingdoms, it was principally in west-central Africa that they experienced the greatest success as both merchants and evangelists.

In 1491 the Kongo king, Mbemba Nzinga a Nkuwu was baptized a Christian by Portuguese missionaries, who renamed him King João I of Kongo. The conversion of João I established Christianity as the official religion of the Kongo court and resulted in numerous conversions of upper-class members of Kongo society. Roman Catholic priests were, from then on, permanently established in the Kongo kingdom. Moreover, a number of those upper-class members of Kongo society traveled to Portugal, where they were received at court and, in some cases, given both secular and religious education. The result of this process of cross-cultural interaction was the creation of a hybrid Portuguese-Kongo culture. Portuguese was spoken at court, and Christianity was adopted not only by the elite but also by ordinary people outside of the capital city, who, whenever possible, underwent Christian baptism and adopted Portuguese names.

The Christianity that was practiced by most Kongolese was strongly tinged by traditional Kongo religious practices, and converts often continued to practice traditional Kongo religion side by side with Christianity. The prevailing opinion was that Roman Catholic priests were powerful medicine men who communicated with an extremely powerful fetish—rather than something of an entirely different order. This hybridization of cultures strongly contributed to what some scholars have identified as "the Charter Generation," a hybridized African-European culture that helps explain the rapidity with which African slaves developed creole cultures and languages in the Americas.

Christianity was deeply culpable in the African slave trade, inasmuch as it consistently provided a moral cloak for the buying and selling of human beings. Contrary to the way that it is popularly imagined, the majority of African slaves were not directly captured by Europeans. With notable exceptions, Europeans simply did not have the naval or military prowess or technology during this period to exercise main force over the strong west and west-central African kingdoms. Slavery was already a endemic throughout Africa, with the enslavement of defeated peoples being common. Fueled by a particularly bellicose period in African history—and the European demand for slaves— many west and west-central African kingdoms, aided by the arms supplied by their European allies, undertook more and more extreme military campaigns, which meant more slaves could be sold to the Americas. It is obvious, then, that both Europeans and Africans were responsible for the Atlantic slave trade, unlike the impression that is created by the trope of European slave raiders with nets.

Nonetheless, Christianity provided the ongoing moral rationale that the enslavement of Africans presented a unique opportunity for evangelization: Europeans could conveniently argue that the temporary evils of slavery were far outweighed when compared with the eternal damnation all nonconverted Africans would experience upon death for having never received Christ. While one can question the extent to which Europeans involved in the slave trade believed, with sincere conviction, that slavery was a moral necessity, many certainly behaved *as if* it were. To this end, the Roman Church provided a vast network of spiritual guardians and religious institutions to support every facet of the slave trade— from royal courts to slave forts, ships, and American destinations. In the slave forts that dotted the African coast, where slaves would wait, sometimes for months, for transport to the Americas, priests often worked as catechists, baptizing and providing religious instruction in a language they barely understood, if at all.

Colonialism and beyond

From the seventeenth to the nineteenth centuries, West and North Africa experienced numerous waves of *jihad* inspired by new forms of radical Islam. Many of these reformist sects were Sufi, driven by a belief that though many rulers were Muslim in name, they were in fact insufficiently pious and often reverted to practicing forms of traditional religion. Additionally, many ascribed to the popular belief that, at the turn of each century, God sends a reformer.

Certainly, one of the most successful of these reformers was Usman dan Fodio, a Fulani Muslim scholar who lived in the predominantly Hausa region of present-day northern Nigeria. Usman dan Fodio was part of the Qadiriyyah sect of Islam, a form of Sufism with reformist leanings. Upset by the oppression he experienced at the hands of Hausa overlords, Usman dan Fodio went into exile with his followers, eventually returning to lead a military campaign that resulted in the founding of the Sokoto Caliphate in the nineteenth century. The Sokoto Caliphate was an Islamic theocracy organized on the basis of Sharia (Islamic law) and had far-reaching influence on the region, resulting in mass conversions and the Islamicization of many of the region's rulers. Although the Sokoto Caliphate ceased to function as an independent state during British colonialism, it exists to this day as a spiritual empire. The present Sultan of Sokoto, a descendent of Usman dan Fodio, is considered the spiritual head of all Nigerian Muslims.

By the middle of the eighteenth century, philanthropists in Europe were writing extensively about the evils of slavery, and they began actively intervening to stop the slave trade. As part of the same impulse to improve the lives of Africans, a flood of Christian missionaries began arriving on the shores of Africa and arguably have never stopped arriving since. These missionaries differed from previous evangelizing efforts in that they were largely independent and did not arrive with merchants, ambassadors, or slave traders.

Among the most important missionary society was the Church Missionary Society (CMS), an evangelical outlet composed predominantly of Anglicans from England. The CMS aimed to convert both Eastern and Western Africa. To say that this new wave of missionaries were not officially an organ of the state is not to say that they were without ulterior motives. Many had quite distinct visions of how to improve the lot of Africans, which often meant making them less African whenever possible and training them to perform menial labor and trades—in other words, to make them into a ready workforce for colonizers and European business interests. This style of missionizing was summarized by the missionary Robert Moffat's slogan, "The Bible and the plow." Moffat was a Congregationalist missionary from the London Missionary Society, another major missionary society that had a particularly strong presence in southern Africa. Moffat's missionary work was conducted in South Africa, where he Christianized and also taught European styles of craftwork and agriculture.

Throughout the nineteenth century, many missionary activities focused on Africans in Sierra Leone and Liberia, where blacks had been "repatriated" by England and the United States. Both countries were founded as places where blacks could return (or, more often, be returned) to Africa. After the abolition of the slave trade in the British Empire in 1807, the British Navy routinely attacked slaving ships from other empires, taking their human cargo to Sierra Leone. Ironically, while this was seen as a repatriation, many of the Africans taken to Sierra Leone were from different parts of the continent—the equivalent of returning Germans to Russia. Liberia, likewise, was founded by American benevolent societies that wished for freed slaves to return to Africa, rather than remain in the United States. While numerous American missionary societies worked tirelessly in Liberia, British missionary societies did the same in Sierra Leone.

In Sierra Leone, the Church Missionary Society established Fourah Bay College in 1827, the first European-style college in West Africa. Founded to train missionaries, Fourah Bay quickly transitioned to being a full-fledged college, which granted degrees through its affiliation with Durham University in England. It was at Fourah Bay that Samuel Ajayi Crowther trained as a priest and was ordained, later to be sent as a missionary to Nigeria. Crowther, who was also a linguist, made enormous strides in developing orthographies and dictionaries for African languages, most especially Yorùbá. Eventually, Crowther was ordained as the first Anglican African bishop when he was installed in 1864 as Bishop of the Niger.

With the introduction of Western styles of education, literacy, and written language, colonial Christianity created a new kind of modernity on the African continent, which was tailored to Christian—but also colonialist—objectives. The importance, in particular, of the CMS schools cannot be overstated. One of the greatest consequences of the missionary encounter was the emergence of a new class of Christian elites, a bourgeoisie that frequently served as colonial administrators under the British indirect system of colonial rule. After African countries achieved independence in the middle of the twentieth century, this Christian elite often became the new de facto governing class.

Although it varied considerably by region and colonial power, Christianity tended to fare much better under colonial rule than did Islam. Perhaps the most notable exception was under French colonial rule, where Islam was indulged while efforts were made to stop the spread of Christianity, which was believed to have greater revolutionary potential. Nevertheless, colonial governments did consistently put a stop to *jihads*. On the other hand, in British colonies, the spread of Islam was actively discouraged—as, for example, in the north of Nigeria, where the Sokoto Caliphate was suppressed and governance by Hausa traditional rulers revived. A notable exception was the success of the unorthodox Islamic sect called Ahmadiyya, which founded a number of schools in Nigeria under colonialism. Because of their orientation toward service and education, they were favored by many West Africans. Over time, however, their heretical claim that their founder, Ahmad, was a messiah and a prophet who came after Muhammed, diminished their popularity, and Muslims were assuaged to support more orthodox interpretations of Islam. Nonetheless, the Ahmadiyya continue to operate in smaller numbers in West Africa.

The indigenization of Christianity in sub-Saharan Africa took place in a number of stages and is an ongoing process to this day. Some of the earliest independent churches were called "Ethiopian" churches—not because they had any actual ties to Ethiopia but because they were tailored specifically to black leadership and made race an issue. On the whole, Ethiopian churches made only cosmetic adjustments to church doctrine and practices; they were notable because they did not depend on white leadership or consider themselves dependents of a larger European ecclesiastic body.

Over time, there emerged African Independent Churches (AIC), founded by Africans who considered themselves to be prophets, often believing that they had been given a vision from God to begin a new church specifically for Africans. The AIC movement is arguably the most creative and vibrant Christian movement in African history and has led to massive numbers of conversions. These churches take African cosmology seriously and make great efforts to root their theologies in terms and practices that make sense to Africans. Also, they tend to place an equal or greater emphasis on the Hebrew scriptures, particularly as a source for belief in prophecy. Most practice faith healing and ecstatic prayer, believe in prophecy and the religious significance of dreams, and see themselves as engaged in a spiritual battle. These churches often include female leadership, and some were founded by women. Often, members of these churches are instantly recognizable by their "uniforms," which typically include dressing all in white. As a rule, their liturgical practices combine both indigenous African rituals and Christian traditions. Examples of African Independent Churches include the Aladura churches, the

Celestial Church of Christ, Christ Apostolic Church, Church of the Lord, and Cherubim and Seraphim, all of which began in Nigeria; the so-called spiritual churches in Ghana; the Zulu Zionist Church in South Africa; and Zimbanguism in the Congo region.

Upon their founding, clashes usually erupted between these new churches and their parent organizations, because they differed in their decision to accommodate African existential and spiritual needs. Indeed, spiritual independence became the central theme in AICs. Although these churches were not involved directly in political liberation, some fervently argued for spiritual liberation from European churches, whose ideologies rejected local African spiritual heritage. Ironically, these same AICs reject indigenous religious practices, deeming them pagan. Thus, there exists a striking ambiguity toward African religions' textures in prophetic churches.

7. A Shembe church ceremony on Palm Sunday, near Durban, South Africa. The Shembe church, also known as the Nazareth Baptist church, is an indigenous African church that borrows from both indigenous Zulu traditions and Christianity.

Pentecostal churches were introduced to Africa in the 1970s, though a few have had long relationships with American and European Pentecostals. They gained more traction in the 1980s and bear close historic ties with the early twentieth-century Azusa Street Revival in the United States. Usually, well-educated people found charismatic churches; their ministers espouse radical spiritual conversion, professing one must be "born again" through baptism of the Holy Spirit. Pentecostal churches seem most identifiable by their beliefs in speaking in tongues, divine healing, and miracles. Furthermore, they often believe that material prosperity signifies God's grace and benevolence. Several churches, therefore, preach what is called a "prosperity gospel," emphasizing the congregation's right to financial freedom. The devil and other evil spirits occupy an equally critical space in Pentecostal theology. Such churches blame the devil and evil spirits for misfortune and other life crises. Many Pentecostal churches believe that generational curses stem from a predecessor's commitment to an African divinity or to an ancestor, entities considered demonic in their theology. Deliverance from curses and demonic possessions becomes one of the minister's main responsibilities.

Charismatic churches share similar worship styles to Pentecostals. Their theologies also bear much in common, so much so that scholars often refer to these denominations as "Pentecostal-charismatic." Like Pentecostals, charismatics pursue physical, spiritual, and emotional healing, they emphasize glossolalia (speaking in tongues) as a manifestation of the Holy Spirit within a person, and they hold the devil and other evil spirits responsible for illness, barrenness, and poverty. Contrary to prophetic churches, charismatics spurn anything related to traditional religions. Importantly, charismatics stand out for their fervent belief in holiness. For some congregations, this involves distinct clothing styles and abstinence from secular media.

Islam also experienced a rapid period of growth and diversification during the early twentieth century, in particular due to the expansion of Sufism across the continent, with Sufi sects such as Tijaniyya and Qaddriyah gaining enormous followings throughout West Africa. The popular appeal of Sufism in Africa is surely related to its ability to incorporate practices that echo traditional African cultural practices and worldviews. Sufis practice charismatic prayer, dance, and music as well as continue to believe in the power of dreams, miraculous healing, and the importance of charismatic leaders. Additionally, Sufism often creates more of a space for the religious lives of women.

By the 1970s, newer forms of fundamentalist Islam waged war against these indigenized Islams. Such campaigns, however, did not succeed everywhere, such as in Senegal, where the Mouride brotherhood was firmly established. Mourides follow the teachings

8. The Grand Mosque in Touba belongs to the Mouride Brotherhood in northern Senegal. The Mourides are a Sufi *tariqa*, a mystical order in West African Islam, which was established by the renowned Sheikh Amadou Bamba. Although the Mourides are largely based in Senegal, their influence has been felt in among African immigrants in such religious urban centers as Paris and New York City.

of Amadou Bamba, a nineteenth-century Senegalese Muslim mystic who emphasized the importance of prayer and work in the lives of the faithful. The popularity of the Mouride brotherhood led to significant transformation in Senegal. Touba, where Bamba was born and the movement began, became a local mecca for pilgrimage and is now the second largest city in Senegal. Furthermore, Mourides have spread through the world, everywhere the Senegalese diaspora has touched—notably in New York City's Harlem, as well as in France and Italy, where they often work as merchants, practicing their unique brand of Muslim "Protestant ethic."

More recently, Wahaabism, a radical, literalistic form of fundamentalist Islam, has spread from Saudi Arabia through trade, diplomacy, and evangelism into much of Africa. It has been instrumental in engineering a radicalization and militarization of Muslim involvement in African public life. In addition, African forms of Pentecostal and charismatic Christianity are also often quite militant. The militarization of both of these forms of fundamentalist religion—Christianity and Islam—has had dire effects on African life, contributing to political instability and endless cycles of preemptive and retributive violence. This dramatic conflict between Christianity and Islam has resulted in changes in indigenous forms of religion, often to the misfortune of the indigenous religions.

Chapter 7
African religions today

Christianity and Islam have been present on the African continent for many centuries, and both are currently enjoying great success. Their good fortune has tended to be the misfortune not only of traditional religions but also a source of envy and conflict between the two traditions. Most African countries won their independence from colonial rule during the early 1960s, and during the period that followed, the new governments often took pains to celebrate and protect traditional religions and values, which were seen as emblems of a uniquely African culture. Perhaps the epitome of this celebration was the Festival of Black Culture and Tradition staged in Nigeria in 1977. Traditional religion provided the vocabulary for a civic religion that grounded patriotism and unification in the collective religious ideology and experience of many African nations. Subsequent decades in many parts of the continent have seen a nearly total collapse of not only traditional/indigenous religions but also social and cultural systems. This included extended family, heath/medicine, and the like, a period that coincidentally corresponds to the increased adoption of radical forms of Christianity and Islam, both of which share the view that traditional religions and their practitioners are pagans and must be expunged from society. Paradoxically, the African elite as well as the state, who had earlier celebrated this cultural heritage, now see these traditions as a major hindrance to social and economic development and to modernization. This is reflected in the postindependence policies on development in several African countries, where the quest for rapid modernization was viewed primarily through the prism of westernization that jettisoned indigenous value systems and knowledge bases.

African myth-historical narratives were not just considered inappropriate for the modern nations, but in fact European Christianity and Middle Eastern culture and Islam were seen as superior to their own local faith traditions. While these radicalized forms of Abrahamic religion battle over who controls the terms of governance and civic life on the continent, the practitioners of traditional religions—and indigenized forms of Christianity and Islam—have tended to get caught in the crossfire, often with tragic consequences. Nevertheless, African religions maintained their identity in modern Africa, and during the last and current centuries they have obtained transnational and global reaches among Euro-American cultures and societies in the New World.

African indigenous religion in contemporary Africa struggles to maintain its legal tone and identity in the face of the forces of Islam and Christianity. Not surprisingly, this battle against indigenous religions has too often resulted in their being seen as no more than superstitions, magic, and fetishist. Rather than religions, practioners of Islam and Christianity now often wrongly view indigenous religions as little more than clandestine practices that one might turn to as an immoral source of power. Thus, one now certainly sees a rise in pseudo-ritual practices and activities in Africa that claim to be traditional religious practices, such as in the ritual killings of albinos reported in certain places in West and East African regions. Similarly, the rise of cult and occult activities among students in Nigerian universities is a clear indication of this new development.

In the Democratic Republic of Congo, witchcraft accusations target street children especially. Changes in the traditional social structure put children in this vulnerable position. The sheer number of orphaned children has strained the extended family social structure due to war, disease, and impoverishment. Children are now viewed as burdens and as threats to the well-being of those who must care for and support them. Consequently, witchcraft and sorcery accusations are on the rise, as discussed in chapter 3, and many evangelical and charismatic churches have special missions organized around fighting witchcraft and delivering suspected witches from such sinful practice.

While practitioners of traditional religions have, in many cases, risen to the defense of their faiths, many suffer a lack of institutional support that has often left them ill-equipped to respond in a way that would successfully perturb the status quo. In some instances, they have adopted some of the vocabulary of the dominant religions. Practitioners of traditional religions will sometimes refer to Christians and Muslims as "unbelievers," a term that they have adopted from these world religions and which is typically leveled against traditionalists. Practitioners of traditional religions who have been educated in a Western model have at times published books about their religious practices, in an attempt to create resources recognizable to Western audiences as religious texts. In the sacred Yorùbá city of Ilé-Ifè, for example, I onced witnessed in the annual festival of Ifá, god of divination, an Ifá choir that wore Christian-style choir robes.

But while African traditional religions are engaged in a battle for their lives on the African continent, they and their sister African diaspora religions are thriving elsewhere in the world—particularly in the Americas and in Europe. Many of these African-derived religions were created by the descendents of Africans who were forcibly brought to the Americas due to the slave trade during the fifteenth to the nineteenth centuries. Over the centuries, they have in many cases developed into traditions that have broad appeal not only to their inheritors but also to a broad range of black, mixed-race, and white peoples. These traditions have increasingly become entwined with present-day African traditional religions, such that it is often no longer easy to tell which is which. Practitioners of Brazilian Candomblé and Cuban Regla de Ocha have extensive relations with African practitioners of modern Yorùbá, Ewe, and Fon religions, and they continue to engage in a dialogue that is at once both generative and tense. While all recognize that they are fundamentally a part of the same family of religious practice, they typically perceive their own practices as the most authentic. Therefore, dialogues have sometimes taken on a didactic tone, which has generated resentment and, on some notable occasions, resulted in a complete collapse of cooperation and civility.

And yet, particularly in the complicated religious terrain of the Americas, these traditions are inextricably bound. The Oyotunji Village, a utopian religious commune founded by African Americans, seeks to emulate as much as possible an idealized vision of precolonial West African life. Practicing what they call "Òrìṣà-Voodoo" (a portmanteau), which combines elements of Yorùbá and Ewe-Fon religions, these African Americans, living in a village in Beaufort County, South Carolina, are in contact with African traditional religionists as well as African American practitioners of African diaspora and African traditional religions. In many respects they see themselves as Africans who are simply living in the United States. While the truth is rather more inflected, it is significant that their vision of African religion in the Americas is essentially utopian and separatist.

On the other hand, many proselytes of African and African diaspora religions in the Americas make every attempt to make these religious practices accessible to the broadest range of people. One of the greatest popularizers of African diaspora religions has been Luisah Teish, an African American woman and priestess of Oshun whose popular books—most especially *Jambalaya* (1988)—combine elements of many African diaspora faiths in a format that emphasizes their efficacy as tools of

9. His Royal Highness, Ọba Ẹ̀funtọlá Oseijeman Adélabú Adéfuńmi I, ruled as Ọba (king) of Oyotunji Village from 1972 to 2005. Oyotunji Village is a utopian community that was founded by Ọba Adéfuńmi I as part of the religious nationalist movements of the twentieth century. Its population has dwindled, but it remains a significant presence in the United States. Here, the Ọba dances to music of the Òrìṣà during an annual festival in Beaufort County, South Carolina.

empowerment for women of color. In a similar vein, Malidoma Patrice Somé, originally from Burkina Faso, has made a career teaching "African shamanism" to American and European clients, who pay to attend his frequent classes, workshops, and retreats. Somé emphasizes that these techniques are still relevant in the modern world and that their meaning is open to everyone, regardless of race, gender, or ethnicity. Both Teish and Somé have been criticized as popularizers who have adulterated the traditions they teach, but they are revered by their students. Regardless of the stance that one takes, the impact that they and others like them are having on the African and African diaspora religious landscape is surely irreversible and likely holds a preview of what is to come.

African diaspora religions

As a striking contrast to the situation in continental Africa, African indigenous religions—or, more accurately, religions inspired by these—in the Americas continue to possess considerable cultural capital. They are, in fact, growing in their number of adherents by the day. African diaspora traditions include Brazilian Candomblé, Cuban Regla de Ocha (less accurately called Santería) and Palo Mayombe, Haitian Vodou, Jamaican Obeah, Trinidadian Orisha and Spiritual Baptist, Carriacou's Big Drum, and North American voodoo, hoodoo, conjure, and ring shouts.

Although widely diverse in their own right, it is possible to speak of certain commonalities that the major traditions—Candomblé, Regla de Ocha, and Vodou—all share. In each case, they are built on two major traditions—European and African—if in fact we may call them traditions. Each is, in itself, a collection of cultural sources competing, in various respects, for dominance.

Given this multitude of sources, it is not surprising that African diasporic traditions are pluralistic by design, a quality that remains one of their greatest strengths and helps to explain their resilience. In many of these traditions, devotees serve multiple deities or spiritual powers, although they recognize the existence and ultimate efficacy of a supreme God. These deities or spirits are variously seen as manifestations of natural phenomena, as ancestors, or as products of mythistorical processes, most notably the creation of the world. They are also emblems of power, spiritual energies that are invoked by their devotees as sources of strength, healing, political legitimacy, and economic liberation. For the descendents of the African slave trade, these religions are reservoirs of cultural memory and also embodied ways to remember slavery. Like devotees of traditional African religions, devotees of African diaspora religions emphasize practice—the enactment of rituals and ceremonies— rather than belief. In these traditions, elements of human playfulness are expressed through dance, music, and decorative arts.

In many respects, these religions function as micro societies, interleaved with—but distinct from—their host societies. They are in dialogue with society but have their own relationships of mutuality, gift-giving, and exchange. In this sense, they are self-reliant, parallel economies, generating their own capitals— economic as well as social, symbolic, cultural, and religious. In many cases this parallel economy is based around services, particularly the healing of various kinds of affliction, physical and spiritual. As in much of West Africa, entrance into the practice of African diaspora religions is often provoked by the onset of mysterious illnesses, ranging from troubling dreams to serious nervous disorders and diseases, which are seen to be caused by spiritual entities. In a sense, this marks the moment at which someone becomes a member of this parallel economy, separated by a step from the main society—in which spirits do not exist to cause spiritual afflictions. As in Africa, the priests and priestesses of these spirit cults are sometimes more effective at curing illness— particularly mental illness—than are Western-trained medical doctors. Haitian Vodou priests and priestesses understand that physical, emotional, and mental illnesses sometimes result from an imbalance in the relationship between the individual and the spirits. Therefore these healers aim to restore right relationships between the sick and the divine.

In many parts of the Americas, these parallel economies, arising from diaspora religions, are so powerful that politicians have attempted to gain prestige through contact with them. In Brazil, several of the most famous Candomblé temples (*terreiros*) in Salvador da Bahia—for example, Ile Ase Opo Afonja and Casa Branca—have become common stopping-grounds for politicians on the campaign trail. In Haiti, the dictator François Duvalier famously recruited Vodou priests as spies and henchmen and used the image of the Tonton Macoute, a boogeyman-like figure from Haitian folklore, as inspiration for the costumes of his secret police. Toward the end of his life as he became more paranoid and reclusive, he began dressing as the Baron, the spiritual master of graveyards, and had his office in the Palais Nationale decorated like a shadowy tomb. Whether Duvalier himself was a practitioner of Vodou is unclear, but he surely understood the power of its cultural caché and attempted to manipulate it to his own power-crazed ends.

In the United States, the famous "voodoo queen" Marie Laveau—whose life and times have recently generated several biographical and pseudo-biographical works—is evidence that this cultural power is nothing new. Although little is known about the specifics of her life, Marie Laveau was a resident of nineteenth-century New Orleans and a free woman of color. She became famous for leading voodoo dances on the outskirts of the city. In addition to her purported spiritual power, through her social influence Laveau is said to have exercised power over the outcomes of court cases and elections. Even in death, two hundred years later, her reputation is so great that people who have never practiced voodoo visit her tomb in Saint Louis Cemetery No. 1 to beg favors of her.

African immigrant religions

Distinct but not entirely separate from African diaspora religions and their practitioners are the religious practices of present-day African immigrants. Since 2001, when I began the African Immigrant Religious Communities Project, I have been involved in examining the presence of African immigrant religious traditions in America. African immigrant religion must be situated within the broader context of cultural and religious pluralism in the United States. These immigrants, many of whom have just escaped dire circumstances, suddenly find themselves in exile, detatched from their communities, languages, and sociocultural milieus. As their numbers in the United States continue to grow, they are making a significant social and cultural impact, especially through the proliferation of religious communities. The 2003 U.S. census estimates that more than one million African-born immigrants were residing in the country, compared with only 230,000 in 1990.

Representing an array of denominations, organizational styles, and sociopolitical concerns, these communities are increasingly visible contributors to religious diversity in North America. The most rapid spread of African immigrant communities is found in gateway cities such as New York, Washington, D.C., Chicago, Atlanta, Houston, Miami, and Los Angeles, as well as in a number of smaller cities and towns such as Lewiston and Portland, both in Maine, and New Brunswick, New Jersey. These communities represent various faith traditions, including Islam (such as the Senegalese Mourides in New York City); mainline Christianity (such as Roman Catholics, Anglicans, Lutherans); Pentecostal/charismatic churches (such as the Redeemed Christian Church of God, the Deeper Life, and the Mountain of Fire Churches); African Initiated Churches (AICs, such as the Church of the Lord [Aladura], Christ Apostolic Church, Celestial Church of Christ); the Ethiopian Churches in Washington, D.C., which seems to be in a separate category of its own; and African indigenous religion.

The vast majority of African Christians, perhaps 80 percent, can be characterized as evangelical. One of the features of these African forms of evangelicalism is the emphasis placed on the need for a conversion experience, to be "born again" in the spirit. This experience is generally not a new conversion to Christianity but a conversion from a "regular" Christian denomination to a more radical form of Christianity—one in which the Bible is identified as the only source of authentic truth and, furthermore, should be interpreted literally. African evangelical churches have embraced the notion that all members are potential "evangelizers" and prospective spreaders of the gospel. Under the guise of bringing the gospel to America and the rest of the world, they encourage members to "plant" new churches wherever they find themselves. They frequently use the language of commerce and also of agriculture (sowing, tilling, toiling, planting) as metaphors for the establishment of new mission posts. Christian African immigrants participate in "reverse missions," defining their mission as a response to the need for the evangelization of Americans who had departed from the faith. It is a reverse of the early evangelization of Africans by Europeans and Americans in the nineteenth and twentieth centuries.

As with diaspora religions, these African immigrant religious communities openly function as parallel, self-reliant societies that fulfill the needs of their members. For many, the imagining of community involves the connection to, and remembrance of, an African homeland. Community members emphasize the importance of speaking their language and hearing it spoken, the chance to enjoy specific delicacies, and the opportunity to sing familiar songs of praise. Services and events often include ethnic markers such as flags and clothing styles, and one often finds reference to cultural beliefs and values (such as respect for elders), which members suggest are defining attributes of their communities.

African immigrant religious communities use numerous formal and informal methods to improve the lives of immigrants, often aimed at both members and nonmembers (such as legal advice, financial assistance, counseling services, support and employment networks). The deep sense of trust that pervades relationships within the religious groups emerges as an important part of their efficacy in addressing immigrant concerns about what are often considered private matters, such as finances or family relationships. These communities provide encouragement for people engaged in an often uphill struggle toward financial security and personal betterment as a well as the hope to sustain their members' efforts.

A significant level of political involvement is found among many first- and second-generation African immigrants. While Barack Obama's rise to political fame is exceptional, it is one instance of a much wider trend. One finds numerous examples of political advocacy by Africans at state and local levels encompassing broad issues of culture, identity, and citizenship. The religious communities have played a central role in shaping political expression, especially through the explicit or implied messages conveyed by leaders and through informal community gatherings (such as in conversation after a service), which often serve as forums for political discussion and debate.

Although African immigrant religious communities seek, in certain respects, to re-create African religious life abroad, there are also significant differences between these American communities and their African "parents." Perhaps the most notable difference is in the role of women. In the United States, it is common to find women in religious communities actively pressing for and gaining a more influential voice. Two notable examples include the Ethiopian communities (both Pentecostal/charismatic and Orthodox) and the African Independent Churches. Transformations in Ethiopian Orthodox religious practice in the American context have meant that women may now chant the mass or *kidase* and are beginning to assume leadership roles in the *kidase* classes. Women comprise the majority within most Celestial Church of Christ congregations in the United States. As a result, many church activities relate to women's experiences such as child-rearing, infertility, and marital counseling. They also include specialized prayers and practices for barren and pregnant women.

In some African Pentecostal churches in the United States, women have begun to serve as head pastors, something that is not common in Africa. Women also are highly involved in transnational religious networks. Women leaders travel worldwide to plant churches, present sermons, and hold seminars. In contrast to ethnic associations, which are in certain cases dominated by men, religion may serve as an important arena in which women can participate equally with men in social and economic projects to benefit the homeland, thereby gaining status and political influence.

As religious communities aim to assist and guide immigrants in their social integration, marriage and the family emerges as a critical arena in the study of religion and gender. In the African immigrant communities, an important factor influencing the family is the increasing work opportunities and incomes of wives in relation to their husbands. As women, many of whom hold skilled positions in the nursing field, become major wage earners in the African immigrant households, a certain level of conflict between husbands and wives has arisen. Although the relationship between employment and women's social and economic autonomy is complex, there is evidence that the increased labor-force opportunities available to African women has elevated their status and strengthened their position in decision making. At the same time, men are faced with the reality that their participation in child care and homemaking is necessary if the household is to function well. Pastors will often base their sermons on the paradox and complexity of living an African marriage in America. While a Pentecostal minister may preach from Saint Paul's epistles that admonish women to obey their husbands, he might also remind the African husbands that "this is America," where there are no maids and servants to do housework, and so the husbands must assist their wives in taking care of household business. Conversely, some African immigrant Christian ministers centralize women's behavior in a patriarchal, biblical perspective of the family. These ministers' churches often provide unique courses for African women in order to anchor their female members in a partriarchal, African culture, which is considered controversial in mainstream American media.

Another important issue for immigrants is the desire to maintain important cultural traditions and identities through transglobal mediums. One indicator among immigrants is a strong desire to be buried in their country of origin. A New York Islamic mosque and a Christian Independent church placed considerable emphasis on providing assistance to pay for the costs of reburial of the deceased in Ghana. These "repatriation" services, the costs of which were viewed as collective in nature, were of essential importance for members of the U.S. immigrant community. It thus confirms that

Africans desire to return to their ancestral home, while alive or after death in old age. Furthermore, it reiterates the point that Africans place strong emphasis on proper burial, which requires contributions from the friends and religious communities of the deceased.

At the same time that these efforts were made to maintain contact with Africa, effort was also often exerted to distinguish religious practices from traditional beliefs. In Washington, D.C., Reverend Aquaowo of Christ Evangelical Ministries spoke out against ancestor worship, arguing that Christians should not place ancestors on the same level as God. At Miracle Fire Ministries, Pastor Lawrence Adetunji and Reverend Adegbile used a handout of weekly "prayer points," called "Breaking the Backbone of Stubborn Witchcraft." According to Reverend Adegbile, this handout was necessary to allow prayer to change belief in witchcraft back to belief in Jesus. This form of Christianity entered the American political arena during the 2008 presidential election when the Kenyan evangelical minister Thomas Muthee, to whom Sarah Palin attributed her success in the Alaskan gubernatorial race, was accused of preaching and praying against witchcraft. The press and Palin's opponents invoked this image to dent her campaign. This was a case of an African priest saying an African prayer in an American Pentecostal church. These ocurrences ultimately point to the dominance of evangelical Christianity among African Christian immigrants and the unforseen consequence of their presence in America today.

Finally, we can also point to a significant diversity in the development of African religious institutions as instruments of mutual aid and support within American civil society. With each immigrant group that has entered the United States, immigrants have developed networks of self-support in employment, housing, and legal assistance. These networks emerged into institutional structures to allocate resources of the state to the groups. Although many of these institutions are less than twenty years old, and therefore their secular functions are in their earliest phases of development, they are working to fill the cultural, social, and economic needs of their communities, providing secular services out of both religious and nonreligious centers. These institutions devote some of their resources and wealth to their members back home and to support indigenous communities in Africa. They are providing language instruction, cultural activities, and access to indigenous healing and religious practices as part of a transglobal identity. Additionally, immigrant communities continue celebrating life stages via naming ceremonies. Parents will name the infant according to their particular ethnic group's customs. If the parents are Christian, they will also perform baptismal rites as prescribed by their denomination. Muslim families will commemorate the child's arrival according to Islamic tradition. Some African immigrant communities also celebrate a young adult's transition from childhood to adulthood. Ghanians in New York, for example, will hold a traditional Akan puberty celebration hosted by women, usually when a girl graduates from high school and is on her way to college.

The new wave of African religions

The past two decades have provided numerous examples of African religions fully entering the global stage, and there is no going back. Take, for example, the ministry of Rev. Sunday Adelaja in Kiev, Ukraine. Adelaja, a Nigerian, initially and somewhat to his dismay found himself in Belarus (then part of the Soviet Union) on a scholarship to study journalism. While in Belarus, Adelaja helped to found a number of underground churches. Deported by the KGB for his religious activities, Adelaja went to Ukraine at the invitation of Jeff Davis, a traveling evangelist who was doing television ministry and needed someone familiar with the language who could represent his interests. From this beginning in Ukraine as a television evangelist, Adelaja began the process of founding churches. In 1994, the first Word of Faith Bible Church was founded. The result is that from his small beginning as the head of a Bible study group, Adelaja now is in charge of the largest church in Ukraine, which has twenty thousand members at its central location and hosts twenty services every Sunday in various auditoriums throughout Kiev. There are hundreds of daughter churches of the Embassy of God—the current name of the church—throughout Ukraine, the former Soviet Union, Europe, the United States, and even Israel. Adelaja is one of the most powerful public figures in Ukraine and is credited, among other things, with aiding in the election of the mayor of Kiev.

The story of Reverend Adelaja is fascinating on a number of levels. First, there is the irony of his ejection from the Soviet Union. Marx's description of religion as the "opiate of the people" is greatly challenged by the story of Adelaja. Communist Russia, purportedly of and for the people, found the sense of agency that Adelaja stirred among Russian peasants to be threatening. This paradox would be funnier if it were not for the tragic circumstances of many people who found their religious lives suppressed under the Soviet system. But this is of minor interest compared with the fact that the most dynamic and powerful religious leader in Ukraine is Nigerian. Ukraine's megachurch is African in origin. It is not too much to say that Adelaja's missionary work has permanently altered the religious landscape of Eastern Europe, instilling African religious sensibilities in a region that had previously been a religious vacuum.

Even the notion of a church on every corner, which has allowed Rev. Sunday Adelaja's church to plant itself in the far corners of the earth and is best exemplified by the Redeem Church, is an idea drawn from these latter days of capitalism. It is the idea of franchise—that people will give you their business if you are where they want it and how they want it. Granted, we are speaking here of spiritual business, but the methods and the outcomes are much the same. One, Matthew Ashimolowo, the founder of Kingsway International Christian Center in East London founded in 1992, is famous for his endorsement of the prosperity gospel—the idea that God's power can help you think yourself rich. He has delivered sermons with names like "Sweatless Wealth." A spiritual message taken from capitalism immediately draws the mind to the prosperity gospel's links with the value of global capitalism.

But if we wish for an example of the dark side of African religion, we need look no further than the case of the so-called Rev. Dr. King—also known as Chukwuemeka Ezeuko—who was sentenced to death in January 2007 for having had six female members of his congregation doused in gasoline and set aflame, which resulted in one woman's death. This came amid other allegations of sexual abuse and harassment of other female members, and his church—the Christian Praying Assembly—seems to have been, quite simply, a cult. His members, who have now mostly abandoned him, thought that he was Jesus. Upon being sentenced to death, King stated, "It is an honour and indeed a privilege to die by hanging as a prophet of God because Jesus Christ was also hanged." So it appears that in addition to being a murderer, King also lacks a solid knowledge of the biblical narrative. Justice Kayode Oyewole, the presiding judge, made the following statement upon condemning King to death: "The variant demonstrated by the accused is a throwback to the dark ages and an assault to the gains attained by humanity in the areas of respect for human dignity, freedom and liberty." I would add that one cannot overlook the irony that Ezeuko chose the name "Rev. Dr. King" after the American civil rights leader who modeled his life after the ideas of pacifism and nonviolence.

African spiritual space is no longer bounded by the African continent. Religiously and spiritually, Africa has absorbed all of the various competing and conflicting messages of the modern world and reflected them back out, boldly, into a new global landscape. For every Adelaja, though, there is also a King. More perplexing is the fact that it is not always obvious which is which—who are the beatified and who are the charlatans. Globalism has opened up a space of possibility in which lunatic religion can thrive, in which a politician—with no consideration for its future impact—will encourage his followers to stone the sinful if it will give him gains at the polls. Some false, charismatic, and unsavory leaders are everywhere ready to dupe, harm, and batter the gullible seeker after religion.

African religious practices in the twenty-first century are booming partly because of the influence of visual and social media. It is not uncommon to hear of online prayer sessions organized by priests in Kenya, Nigeria, and the United States. These prayer sessions create communities of cyberspace worshippers, united in the common purpose of sharing fervent prayers that address existential and daily concerns of devotees. Attracting millions of worshippers who join in marathon daily prayers, weekly praise and worship sessions, monthly and yearly conventions and revival meetings, these new cyber methods encourage millions of devotees from across the globe to participate in the traditions. While Christianity certainly takes center stage in this form of cyber religiosity, African indigenous religion also features prominently in it. In the United States, Europe, and Asia, many priests of Yorùbá òrìṣà and Ifá traditions have created houses of worship that make use of these new technologies for devotional practices. Since the late twentieth century, African religions have assumed a new identity as a transnational and global religion.

In a world of increasing globalization, from which Africa is not exempt—far from it as Africa is often the unwitting center—we must expand our focus in order to recognize satellite and even fringe religious expressions as part and parcel of the African religious experience in toto. Granted, we should not say that Vodou, Candomblé, Santería, and the like *are* African religions, per se. They are equally, if not more so, what J. Lorand Matory calls "Black Atlantic religions." In addition, Euro-American religions have also become Africanized. The Church of Latter-Day Saints in central Ilé-Ifẹ̀, Nigeria, is as African as the Ifá divination temple on the ancient sacred hill of Oke Ìtasè, Ilé-Ifẹ̀. We must understand these examples as integral to the same religious trajectory and spiritual mosaic that Africans, Europeans, and Americans participate in with the same vigor and deep sense of devotion. If, in our world of increasingly hyphenated and hybrid identities, it has become more challenging to say what African religion *is*, it has become perhaps even more challenging to say for certain what it *isn't*. If we look more carefully, we find manifestations of it everywhere.

References

Preface

Jan Platvoet, James Cox, and Jacob Olupọna, eds., *The Study of Religions in Africa: Past, Present and Prospects* (Cambridge, UK: Roots and Branches, 1996).

Joseph Conrad, *Heart of Darkness* (Richmond, VA: Oneworld Classics, 2009).

Sarkozy quotations from Diadie Ba, "Africans Still Seething Over Sarkozy Speech," *Reuters* (September 5, 2007), http://uk.reuters.com/article/2007/09/05/uk-africa-sarkozy-idUKL0513034620070905.

Mircea Eliade's description of indigenous spirituality from Eliade, *The Myth of Eternal Return: Cosmos and History* (Princeton, NJ: Princeton University Press, 2005), 86.

Chapter 1

Description of the Ndembu of Zambia from Victor Turner, *The Drums of Affliction: A Study of Religious Processes Among the Ndembu of Zambia* (London: International African Institute, 1968), 52–53.

Descriptions of the Bambara of Mali from Clyde W. Ford, *The Hero with an African Face: Mythic Wisdom of Traditional Africa* (New York: Bantam, 1999), 179–81.

Statement about the BaKongo beliefs from Kimbwandende Kia Bunseki Fu-Kiau, *African Cosmology of the Bântu-Kôngo: Tying the Spiritual Knot—Principles for Life and Living*, 2nd ed. (Brooklyn, NY: Athelia Henrietta Press, Publishing in the Name of Orunmila, 2001), 21.

Romanian historian's argument from Mircea Eliade, *The Myth of the Eternal Return: Cosmos and History*, trans. Willard R. Trask (Princeton, NJ: Princeton University Press, 2005), 74–75.

Analysis of African myths from Michael D. Jackson, *Minima Ethnographica: Intersubjectivity and the Anthropological Project* (Chicago: University of Chicago Press, 1998), 118–22.

Hutu historical myths from Liisa Malkki, *Purity and Exile: Violence, Memory, and National Cosmology Among Hutu Refugees in Tanzania* (Chicago: University of Chicago Press, 1995), 59–70.

Chapter 2

Driberg, J. H. *The Lango: A Nilotic Tribe of Uganda* (London: T. F. Unwin, 1923), 223.

Ovambo people from Teddy Aarni, *The Kalunga Concept in Ovambo Religion from 1870 Onwards* (Stockholm: University of Stockholm: Almquist and Wiksell [distributors], 1982), 15.

Statements about Beng people of Côte d'Ivoire from Alma Gottlieb, *The Afterlife Is Where We Come From: The Culture of Infancy in West Africa* (Chicago: University of Chicago Press, 2004), 78, 86–87, 98, 162.

BaKongo people's beliefs about water spirits from Wyatt MacGaffey, *Kongo Political Culture: The Conceptual Challenge of the Particular* (Bloomington: Indiana University Press, 2000), 27, 123.

Statements about the god Tongnaab from Jean Allman and John Parker, *Tongnaab: The History of a West African God* (Bloomington: Indiana University Press, 2005), 1–181.

Chapter 3

Description of king's relationship with ancestors from Serge Tcherkézoff, *Dual Classification Reconsidered: Nyamwezi Sacred Kingship and Other Examples*, trans. Martin Thom (Cambridge: Cambridge University Press, 1987), 69–75.

Description of why the king eats only after sunset, Werner Lange, *Dialectics of Divine "Kingship" in the Kafa Highlands*, Occasional Paper No. 15 (Los Angeles: African Studies Center, University of California, 1976), 3–4, 25–26, 28–33.

Sukuma belief about mediumistic divination from Koen Stroeken, "'Stalking the Stalker': A Chwezi Initiation into Spirit Possession and Experiential Structure," *Journal of the Royal Anthropological Institute (N.S.)* 12 (2006): 785–802.

Clairvoyance of *laibon* from Elliot Fratkin, "The Laibon Diviner and the Healer among Samburu Pastoralists of Kenya," in *Divination and Healing: Potent Vision*, ed. Michael Winkelman and Philip M. Peek (Tucson: University of Arizona Press, 2004), 207–26.

Yaka worldview from René Devisch, "Yaka Divination: Acting out the Memory of Society's Life-Spring," in Winkelman and Peek, *Divination and Healing*, 243–63.

Description of Regional Pastor from John M. Janzen and Wyatt MacGaffey, *An Anthology of Kongo Religion: Primary Texts from Lower Zaïre* (Lawrence: University Press of Kansas, 1974), 75–77.

Description of diviner from Susan Reynolds Whyte, "Knowledge and Power in Nyole Divination," in *African Divination Systems: Ways of Knowing*, ed. Philip M. Peek (Bloomington: Indiana University Press, 1991), 153–71.

Ifá and *Pa* systems from Umar Habila Dadem Danfulani, "*Pa* Divination: Ritual Performance and Symobolism among the Ngas, Mupun, and Mwaghavul of the Jos Plateau, Nigeria," in *African Spirituality: Forms, Meanings, and Expressions*, ed. Jacob K. Olupona (New York: Crossroad, 2000), 87–111.

Arabic geomancy, Wim Van Binsbergen, "Regional and Historical Connections of Four-Tablet Divination in Southern Africa," *Journal of Religion in Africa* 25, no. 1 (1996): 2–29.

Zanahary from Robert W. and Linda K. Sussman, "Divination among the Sakalava of Madagascar," in *Extrasensory Ecology: Parapsychology and Anthropology*, ed. Joseph K. Long (Metuchen, NJ: Scarecrow, 1977), 271–91.

Mami Wata devotees in Venise N. Battle, "Mami Wata in Saced Mode: Epistemological Concerns in the Study of an African God/dess" (master's thesis, Harvard Divinity School, 2010), 44.

Kgaga belief in women's supernatural powers, W. D. Hammond-Tooke, *Boundaries and Belief: Structure of a Sotho Worldview* (Johannesburg, South Africa: Witwatersrand University Press, 1981), 95–101.

Lozi claims about witches and sorcerers, Victor Turner, *The Lozi Peoples of North-western Rhodesia* (London: International African Institute, 1968), 51–52.

Tsav as a physical substance around the heart, Joseph S. Gbenda, "Witchcraft as a Double-Edged Sword in Tiv Traditional Society," *Aquinas Journal* 1, no. 1 (2008): 89–98.

References

Mura of Déla ethnographic work in northern Cameroon, Diane Lyons, "Witchcraft, Gender, Power and Intimate Relations in Mura Compounds in Déla, Northern Cameroon," *World Archeology* 29, no. 3 (1998): 344–62.

Male witches, Ralph A. Austen, "The Moral Economy of Witchcraft: an Essay in Comparative History," in *Modernity and Its Malcontents: Ritual and Power in Postcolonial Africa*, ed. Jean Comaroff and John. L. Comaroff (Chicago: University of Chicago Press, 1993), 91.

Witch-hunting to political and economic disenfranchisement and to youth agency, Isak A. Niehaus, "Witch-hunting and Political Legitimacy: Continuity and Change in Green Valley, Lebowa," *Africa* 63, no. 4 (1993): 498–529.

Chapter 4

Discussion on *Tumdo* or "male initiation" and the roles females play in the rituals among the Nadi of Kenya, Myrtle S. Langley, *The Nandi of Kenya: Life Crisis in a Period of Change* (New York: St. Martin's Press, 1979), 18–45.

Discussion on transition from boyhood to manhood by the Nyae Nyae !Kung in Namibia, Lorna J. Marshall, *Nyae Nyae !Kung Beliefs and Rites* (Cambridge, MA: Peabody Museum of Archaeology and Ethnology, Harvard University, 1999), 203–20.

Dipo, a female initiatory rite among Krobo women in Ghana, Marijke Steegstra, *Resilient Rituals: Krobo Initiation and the Politics of Culture in Ghana* (Münster: Lit, 2004), 241–84.

Rainmaking rituals among the Chewa of Mozambique and *buna galla* sacrificial ritual among the Wasa Boorana of East Africa, Catherine Bell, *Ritual: Perspectives and Dimensions* (New York: Oxford University Press, 1997), 102–8; J. W. M. van Breuge, *Chewa Traditional Religion* (Blantyre, Malawi: Christian Literature Association in Malawi, 2001), 43–72; Mario I. Aguilar, *The Politics of God in East Africa: Oromo Ritual and Religion* (Trenton, NJ: Red Sea Press, 2009), 33–54.

Rain rites among the Ihanzu of Tanzania, Todd Sanders, *Beyond Bodies: Rainmaking and Sense Making in Tanzania* (Toronto: University of Toronto Press, 2008), 128–31.

Mortuary practices among the Bunyoro of Western Uganda, J. H. M. Beattie, "Nyoro Mortuary Rites," *Uganda Journal* 25, no. 2 (1961): 171–83.

Zulu marriage rituals, Max Kohler and N. J. V. Warmelo, *Marriage Customs in Southern Natal* (Pretoria: Government Printer, 1933), 47–65; E. Thomas Lawson, "The Zulu and Their Religious Tradition." *Religious Traditions of the World: a Journey Through Africa, North America, Mesoamerica, Judaism, Christianity, Islam, Hinduism, Buddhism, China, and Japan*, ed. H. Byron Earhart (San Francisco: HarperSanFrancisco, 1993), 29–58.

Xhosa (South Africa) beer-drinking rituals, Patrick A. McAllister, *Xhosa Beer Drinking Rituals: Power, Practice and Performance in the South African Rural Periphery* (Durham, NC: Carolina Academic Press, 2006), 19–41, 107–51, 201–25.

Òsun festival of Òsogbo, Nigeria, Diedre L. Bádéjo, *Osun Seegesi: The Elegant Deity of Wealth, Power, and Femininity* (Trenton, NJ: Africa World Press, 1996), 103–22.

Iden festival in Nigeria, Yomi Akinyeye, "Iden Festival: Historical Reconstruction from Ceremonial Reenactment," *Orisa: Yorubu Gods and Spiritual Identity in Africa and the Diaspora*, ed. Toyin Falola, and Ann Genova (Trenton, NJ: Africa World Press, 2006), 87–102.

Chapter 5

Quote on the *boli* sculptures of the Bamana, Sarah Brett-Smith, "The Poisonous Child," *RES: Anthropology and Aesthetic* 6 (1983): 47–64.

The Fang of southern Cameroon and Gabon employment of wooden statues as reliquary guards, Roy Sieber and Roslyn Adele Walker, *African Art in the Cycle of Life* (Washington, DC: National Museum of African Art, Smithsonian Institution Press, 1988), 139.

The Bwa's elaborately carved animal-inspired masks thought to bring fertility to crops, John W. Nunley, "West African Sculpture: Sacred Space, Spirit, and Power," *Bulletin (St. Louis Art Museum)*, New Series 16, no. 4 (1983): 1–41.

The celebration of women in the Gèlèdè festival of the Yorùbá of Nigeria, Henry John Drewal and Margaret Thompson Drewal, *Gelede: Art and Female Power among the Yoruba* (Bloomington: Indiana University Press, 1990), 17–37, 62–105.

Women of the Sande secret societies of the Mende, Ruth B. Phillips, *Representing Woman: Sande Masquerades of the Mende of Sierra Leone* (Los Angeles: UCLA Fowler Museum of Cultural History, 1995), 113–37; Sylvia Boone, *Radiance from the Waters: Ideals of*

Feminine Beauty in Mende Art (New Haven, CT: Yale University Press, 1986), 39; Benjamin C. Ray, *African Religions: Symbol, Ritual, and Community*, 2nd ed. (Upper Saddle River, NJ: Prentice Hall, 2000), 118–20.

Quote on the supernatural power of the Mano of Liberia masks, Monica Blackmun Visonà, Robin Poynor, and Herbert M. Cole, *History of Art in Africa* (New York: Abrams, 2001), 184, 190.

Statement on African masquerades incorporating masks representing colonists and foreigners, Fritz Kramer, *The Red Fez: Art and Spirit Possession and Africa*, trans. Malcolm Green (London: Verso, 1993), 138–78.

Discussion of Zulu and Xhosa beads adorning clothing, Gary van Wyk, "Illuminated Signs. Style and Meaning in the Beadwork of the Xhosa- and Zulu Speaking Peoples," *African Arts* 36, no. 3 (2003): 12–33, 93–94.

Example of beads used on the throne and footstool of the king of the Bamum, Christraud Geary, "Bamum Thrones and Stools," *African Arts* 14, no. 4 (1981): 32–43, 87–88.

Discussion on African traditional cultures as oral in nature, divine inspiration, divination, and quote about the Dinka of Sudan, Philip Peek "The Power of Words in African Verbal Arts," *Journal of American Folklore* 94, no. 371 (1981): 19–43; *Divination and Healing: Potent Vision*, ed. Michael Winkelman and Philip M. Peek (Tucson: University of Arizona Press, 2004), 243–63.

Discussion on statues of sacrificial victims unearthed in Ilé-Ifè, Frank Willett, *Ife in the History of West African Sculpture* (New York: McGraw-Hill, 1967), 68–69.

Discussion on the intersection between Mende female beauty standards and religious ideals, Sylvia Boone, *Radiance from the Waters: Ideals of Feminine Beauty in Mende Art* (New Haven, CT: Yale University Press, 1986), 129–36.

Chapter 6

Discussion on Christianity entering the African continent via the Roman Empire, Funso Afolayan, "Civilizations of the Upper Nile and North Africa," in *Africa*, vol. 1, *African History before 1885*, ed. Toyin Falola (Durham, NC: Carolina Academic Press, 2000), 73–110.

Examples of indigenous religious practices and rituals changing over time due to Christian and Islamic influences, William B. Anderson and Ogbu U. Kalu, "Christianity in Sudan and Ethiopia," in *African Christianity: An African Story*, ed. Ogbu U. Kalu (Trenton, NJ: Africa World Press, 2007), 66–99.

Discussions on King Ezana's conversion to Christianity, Niall Finneran, *The Archaeology of Christianity in Africa* (Charleston, SC: Tempus, 2002), 125; Ephraim Issac, *The Ethiopian Orthodox Tawahido Church* (Trenton: NJ: Africa World Press/Red Sea Press, 2012), 18–20.

History on introduction of Islam to West Africa and example of the chief of the Barghawata developing a new religion by scripting a Qur'an in Berber, M. El Fasi and I. Hrbek, "Stages in the Development of Islam and Its Dissemination in Africa," in *General History of Africa 3: Africa from the Seventh to the Eleventh Century*, ed. M. El Fasi and I. Hrbek (Berkeley: University of California Press, UNESCO, 1988), 57–91.

Discussion on the amulets worn by contemporary African Muslims, René A. Bravmann, "Islamic Art and Material Culture in Africa," in *The History of Islam in Africa*, ed. Nehemia Levtzion and Randall Lee Pouwels (Athens: Ohio University Press, 2000), 489–518.

Discussion on "the Charter Generation" as a hybridized African-European culture, Ira Berlin, *Many Thousands Gone: The First Two Centuries of Slavery in North America* (Cambridge: MA: Belknap Press, 1998), 15–77; Linda M. Heywood and John K. Thornton, *Central Africans, Atlantic Creoles, and the Foundation of the Americas, 1585–1660* (Cambridge: Cambridge University Press, 2007), 238.

Example of Pentecostal church belief of generational curses, J. Kwabena Asamoah-Gyadu, "Mission to 'Set the Captives Free': Healing, Deliverance, and Generational Curses in Ghanaian Pentecostalism," *International Review of Missions* 93, no. 370–71 (2004), 389–406.

Chapter 7

Discussion on witchcraft accusations targeted at children, Danielle Marie Gram, "Child Witches and Witch Hunt: New Images of the Occult in the Democratic Republic of Congo" (BA thesis, Harvard University, 2011).

Discussion on the Ọ̀yọ́túnjí Village founded by African Americans, Kamari Maxine Clarke, *Mapping Yorùbá Networks: Power and*

Agency in the Making of Transnational Communities (Durham, NC: Duke University Press, 2004), 51–59.

Haitian Vodou priests and priestesses, Karen McCarthy Brown, "Afro-Caribbean Spirituality: A Haitian Case Study," in *Healing and Restoring: Health and Medicine in the World's Religions Traditions*, ed. Lawrence E. Sullivan (New York: Collier Macmillan, 1989), 255–85.

Discussion about an African priest saying an African prayer in an American Pentecostal church, quote by Jacob Olupọna stated in Jessica Fargen, "Palin 'Witchcraft' Flap All Smoke, No Fire," *Boston Herald*, September 26, 2008, sec. 5.

Discussion about Rev. Sunday Adelaja, "Minister Information, Pastor Sunday Adelaja, It is Easy Ministries," www.it-iseasy.org/contact/friends/sunday.php; Jacob Olupọna, "On Africa, a Need for Nuance," *Harvard Divinity Bulletin* 35, no. 4 (Autumn 2007); Laura Peek, "Prosperity Is the Promise of God," *Times Online (England)*, March 16, 2003, http://www.thetimes.co.uk/tto/news/uk/article1907850.ece.

Discussion about Rev. Dr. King/Chukwuemeka Ezeuko, "Preacher to Hang for Sin Burnings," *British Broadcasting Corporation Online*, January 11, 2007, http://news.bbc.co.uk/2/hi/africa/6252463.stm; "Court Sentences Rev. King to Death by Hanging," www.gamji.com.

Further reading

Abdullah, Zain. *Black Mecca: The African Muslims of Harlem*. Oxford: Oxford University Press, 2010.

Abiodun, Rowland. *"What Follows Six Is More than Seven": Understanding African Art*. London: British Museum Department of Ethnography, 1995.

Afolayan, Funso. "Civilizations of the Upper Nile and North Africa." In *Africa*. Vol. 1, *African History before 1885*, edited by Toyin Falola, 73–110. Durham, NC: Carolina Academic Press, 2000.

"Africa, West." In *New International Dictionary of Pentecostal and Charismatic Movements*, edited by Stanley M. Burgess and Eduard M. van der Maas, 11–21. Rev. ed. Grand Rapids, MI: Zondervan, 2002.

"African religions." In *Wordsworth Dictionary of Beliefs and Religions*, edited by Rosemary Goring, 7–8. Herefordshire: Wordsworth Reference, 1992.

Aguilar, Mario I. *The Politics of God in East Africa: Oromo Ritual and Religion*. Trenton, NJ: Red Sea Press, 2009.

Allman, Jean, and John Parker. *Tongnaab: The History of a West African God*. Bloomington: Indiana University Press, 2005.

Anderson, William B., and Ogbu U. Kalu. "Christianity in Sudan and Ethiopia." In *African Christianity: An African Story*, edited by Ogbu U. Kalu. Trenton, NJ: Africa World Press, 2007.

Arohunmolase, Lawrence Oyewole. "Spirit Possession in the Egba Festival." In *Orisa: Yoruba Gods and Spiritual Identity in Africa and the Diaspora*, edited by Toyin Falola and Ann Genova, 103–12. Trenton, NJ: Africa World Press, 2006.

Akinyeye, Yomi. "Iden Festival: Historical Reconstruction from Ceremonial Reenactment." In Falola and Genova, *Orisa*, 87–102. Trenton: Africa World Press, 2006.

Anderson, William B., and Ogbu U. Kalu. "Christianity in Sudan and Ethiopia." In *African Christianity: An African Story*, edited by Ogbu U. Kalu, 67–101. Trenton, NJ: Africa World Press, Inc., 2007.

Apter, Andrew. *Beyond Words: Discourse and Critical Agency in Africa*. Chicago: University of Chicago Press, 2007.

Ardner, Edwin. *Kingdom on Mount Cameroon: Studies in the History of the Cameroon Coast 1500-1970*. Providence, RI: Berghahn, 1996.

Asamoah-Gyadu, J. Kwabena. "Mission to 'Set the Captives Free': Healing, Deliverance, and Generational Curses in Ghanaian Pentecostalism." *International Review of Missions* 93, no. 370–71 (2004): 389–406.

Austen, Ralph A. "The Moral Economy of Witchcraft: An Essay in Comparative History." In *Modernity and Its Malcontents: Ritual and Power in Postcolonial Africa*, edited by Jean Comaroff and John L. Comaroff, 89–110. Chicago: University of Chicago Press, 1993.

Ba, Diadie. "Africans Still Seething over Sarkozy Speech." *Reuters*, September 5, 2007, http://uk.reuters.com/article/2007/09/05/uk-africa-sarkozy-idUKL0513034620070905.

Badejo, Diedre L. *Osun Seegesi: The Elegant Deity of Wealth, Power, and Femininity*. Trenton, NJ: Africa World Press, 1996.

Barnes, Cedric. "Ibadis." In *Medieval Islamic Civilization: An Encyclopedia*, edited by Josef W. Meri, 341–42. New York: Routledge, 2006.

Battle, Venise N. "Mami Wata in Saced Mode: Epistemological Concerns in the Study of an African God/dess." M.T.S. thesis. Harvard Divinity School, 2010.

Beattie, J. H. M. *Bunyoro: an African Kingdom*. New York: Holt, 1960.

Beattie, J. H. M. *Understanding an African Kingdom: Bunyoro*. New York: Holt, Reinhart, and Winston, 1965.

Bell, Catherine. *Ritual: Perspectives and Dimensions*. New York: Oxford University Press, 1997.

Berlin, Ira. *Many Thousands Gone: The First Two Centuries of Slavery in North America*. Cambridge, MA: Belknap Press, 1998.

Berns, Marla C. "Ga'anda Scarification: A Model for Art and Identity." In *Marks of Civilization: Artistic Transformations of the Human Body*, edited by Arnold Rubin, 57–76. Los Angeles: Museum of Cultural History, University of California, Los Angeles, 1988.

Bongmba, Elias K. *The Wiley-Blackwell Companion to African Religions*. Altrium, UK: John Wiley & Sons, 2012.

Boone, Sylvia. *Radiance from the Waters: Ideals of Feminine Beauty in Mende Art*. New Haven: Yale University Press, 1986.

Bourgeois, Arthur P. *Art of the Yaka and Suku*. Mendon, France: A. & F. Chaffin, 1984.

Bradbury, R. E. *The Benin Kingdom and the Edo-speaking Peoples of South-Western Nigeria*. Ethnographic Survey of Africa Series Western Africa, part 13. London: International African Institute, 1957.

Bravmann, René A. *African Islam*. Washington, DC: Smithsonian Institution Press, 1983.

Bravmann, Renée A. "Islamic Art and Material Culture in Africa." In *The History of Islam in Africa*, edited by Nehemia Levtzion and Randall Lee Pouwels, 489–518. Athens: Ohio University Press, 2000.

Brett-Smith, Sarah. "The Poisonous Child." *RES: Anthropology and Aesthetics* 6 (1983): 47–64.

Breugel, J. W. M. van. *Chewa Traditional Religion*. Blantyre, Malawi: Christian Literature Association in Malawi, 2001.

Brown, Karen McCarthy. "Afro-Caribbean Spirituality: A Haitian Case Study." In *Healing and Restoring: Health and Medicine in the World's Religions Traditions*, edited by Lawrence E. Sullivan, 255–85. New York: Collier Macmillan, 1989.

Clarke, Kamari Maxine. *Mapping Yoruba Networks: Power and Agency in the Making of Transnational Communities*. Durham, NC: Duke University Press, 2004.

Danfulani, Umar Habila Dadem. "*Pa* Divination: Ritual Performance and Symobolism among the Ngas, Mupun, and Mwaghavul of the Jos Plateau, Nigeria." In *African Spirituality: Forms, Meanings, and Expressions*, edited by Jacob K. Olupona, 87–111. New York: Crossroad Publishing, 2000.

Devisch, René. "Yaka Divination: Acting out the Memory of Society's Life-Spring." In *Divination and Healing: Potent Vision*, edited by Michael Winkelman and Philip M. Peek, 243–63. Tucson: University of Arizona Press, 2004.

Drewal, Henry John, and Margaret Thompson Drewal. *Gelede: Art and Female Power among the Yoruba*. Bloomington: Indiana University Press, 1990.

Driberg, J. H. *The Lango: a Nilotic Tribe of Uganda*. London: T. F. Unwin, 1923.

Dundas, Charles. *Kilimanjaro and Its People: A History of the Wachagga, Their Laws, Customs, and Legends, Together with Some Account of the Highest Mountain in Africa*. London: H. F.& G. Witherby, 1924.

Dupré, Wilhelm. *Religion in Primitive Cultures: A Study in Ethnophilosophy*. Religion and Reason 9. The Hague: Mouton, 1975.

Ebong, Inih A. "The Aesthetics of Ugliness in Ibibio Dramatic Arts." *African Studies Review* 38, no. 3 (1995): 43–59.

Eglash, Ron. "Bamana Sand Divination: Recursion in Ethnomathematics." *American Anthropologist*, New Series 99, no. 1(1997): 112–22.

El Fasi, M., and I. Hrbek. "Stages in the Development of Islam and Its Dissemination in Africa." In *General History of Africa*. Vol. 3, *Africa from the Seventh to the Eleventh Century*, edited by M. El Fasi and I. Hrbek, 57–91. London: Berkeley, 1988.

Eliade, Mircea. *The Myth of Eternal Return: Cosmos and History*. Translated by Willard R. Trask. Bollingen Series 46. Princeton, NJ: Princeton University Press, 1971.

Ellis, Stephen, and Gerrie Ter Haar. *Worlds of Power: Religious Thought and Political Practice in Africa*. London: Hurst, 2004.

Ephirim-Donkor, Anthony. *African Spirituality: On Becoming Ancestors*. Trenton, NJ: Africa World Press, 1997.

Fargen, Jessica. "Palin 'Witchcraft' Flap All Smoke, No Fire." *Boston Herald*, September 26, 2008: 5.

Ford, Clyde W. *The Hero with an African Face: Mythic Wisdom of Traditional Africa*. New York: Bantam, 1999.

Fratkin, Elliot. "The Laibon Diviner and the Healer among Samburu Pastoralists of Kenya." In Winkelman and Peek, *Divination and Healing*, 207–26.

Friedson, Steven M. *Remains of Ritual: Northern Gods in a Southern Land*. Chicago: University of Chicago Press, 2009.

Fu-Kiau, Kimbwandende Kia Bunseki. *African Cosmology of the Bântu-Kôngo: Tying the Spiritual Knot—Principles of Life and Living*. 2nd ed. Brooklyn, NY: Athelia Henrietta Press, Publishing in the Name of Orunmila, 2001.

Gbenda, Joseph S. "Witchcraft as a Double-Edged Sword in Tiv Traditional Society." *Aquinas Journal* 1, no. 1 (2008): 89–98.

Geary, Christraud. "Bamum Thrones and Stools." *African Arts* 14, no. 4 (1981): 32–43, 87–88.

"German Discovers Atlantis in Africa: Leo Frobenius Says Find of Bronze Poseidon Fixes Lost Continent's Place." *New York Times*, January 30, 1911.

Gilbert, Michelle. "Akan Terracotta Heads: Gods or Ancestors?" *African Arts* 22, no. 4 (1989): 34–43, 85–66.

Glasse, Cyril. *The New Encyclopedia of Islam.* 3rd ed. Lanham, MD: Rowman & Littlefield, 2008.

Glaze, Anita J. "Call and Response: A Senufo Female Caryatid Drum." *Art Institute of Chicago Museum Studies* 19, no. 2 (1980): 118–33, 196–98.

Gottlieb, Alma. *The Afterlife Is Where We Come From: The Culture of Infancy in West Africa.* Chicago: University of Chicago Press, 2004.

Gram, Danielle. "Child Witches and Witch Hunt: New Images of the Occult in the Democratic Republic of Congo." BA honors thesis, Harvard University, 2011.

Green, December. *Gender Violence in Africa: African Women's Responses.* New York: St. Martin's, 1999.

Griaule, Marcel. *Conversations with Ogotemêli: An Introduction to Dogon Religious Ideas.* London: Published for the International African Institute by Oxford University Press, 1965.

Hallen, B., and J. O. Sodipo. *Knowledge Belief & Witchcraft: Analytic Experiments in African Philosophy.* London: Ethnographica, 1986.

Hammond-Tooke, W. D. *Boundaries and Belief: The Structure of a Sotho Worldview.* Johannesburg: Witwatersrand University Press, 1981.

Heywood, Linda M., and John K. Thornton. *Central Africans, Atlantic Creoles, and the Foundation of the Americas, 1585–1660.* Cambridge: Cambridge University Press, 2007.

Hodgson, Janet. *The God of the Xhosa: A Study of the Origins and Development of the Traditional Concepts of the Supreme Being.* Cape Town: Oxford University Press, 1982.

Homberger, Lorenz. "Where the Mouse Is Omniscient: The Mouse Oracle among the Guro." In *Insight and Artistry in African Divination,* edited by John Pemberton III, 157–67. Washington, DC: Smithsonian Institution, 2000.

Hucks, Tracey. *Yoruba Traditions and African American Religious Nationalism.* Albuquerque: University of New Mexico Press, 2013.

Isichei, Elizabeth. *A History of Christianity in Africa: From Antiquity to the Present.* Grand Rapids, MI: Eerdmans, 1995.

Isichei, Elizabeth. *A History of Nigeria.* London: Longman, 1983.

Jackson, Michael. *Minima Ethnographica: Intersubjectivity and the Anthropological Project.* Chicago: University of Chicago Press, 1998.

Jalobo, Jacan Ngomlokojo. *Rituals of Religious Worship among the Traditional Alur.* Gulu, Uganda: Jalobo Jacan Ngomlokojo, 1985.

Janzen, John M., and Wyatt MacGaffey. *An Anthology of Kongo Religion: Primary Texts from Lower Zaïre*. Lawrence: University of Kansas, 1974.

Kalu, Ogbu U. *African Pentecostalism: An Introduction*. Oxford: Oxford University Press, 2008.

King, Noel Q. *African Cosmos: An Introduction to Religion in Africa*. Belmont: Wadsworth Publishing Company, 1986.

Kipury, Naomi. *Oral Literature of the Maasai*. Nairobi: Heinemann Educational Books, 1983.

Knappert, Jan. *Bantu Myths and Other Tales—Collected and Translated from the Bantu*. Leiden: E. J. Brill, 1977.

Knappert, Jan. *Namibia: Land and Peoples, Myths and Fables*. Leiden: E.J. Brill, 1981.

Kohler, Max. *Marriage Customs in Southern Natal*. Edited by N. J. van Warmelo. Pretoria: Government Printer, 1933.

Kramer, Fritz. *The Red Fez: Art and Spirit Possession and Africa*. Translated by Malcolm Green. London: Verso, 1993.

Lange, Werner. *Dialectics of Divine "Kingship" in the Kafa Highlands*. Occasional Paper No. 15. Los Angeles: African Studies Center, University of California, 1976.

Langely, Myrtle S. *The Nandi of Kenya: Life Crisis Rituals in a Period of Change*. New York: St. Martin's, 1979.

Larson, Pier Martin. "Austronesian Mortuary Ritual in History: Transformations of Secondary Burial (Famadihana) in Highland Madagascar." *Ethnohistory* 48, nos. 1–2 (2001): 123–55.

Lawson, E. Thomas. "The Zulu and Their Religious Tradition." In *Religious Traditions of the World: A Journey Through Africa, North America, Mesoamerica, Judaism, Christianity, Islam, Hinduism, Buddhism, China, and Japan*, edited by H. Byron Earhart, 29–58. San Francisco: HarperSanFrancisco, 1993.

Leib, Elliot, and Renee Romano. "Reign of the Leopard: Ngbe Ritual." *African Arts* 18, no. 1 (1984): 48–57, 94–96.

Lewis, J. Murphy. *Why Ostriches Don't Fly and Other Tales from the African Bush*. Englewood, CO: Libraries Unlimited, 1997.

Lloyd, P. C. "Sacred Kingship and Government among the Yoruba." In *Africa and Change*, edited by Collin M. Turnbull, 289–309. New York: Knopf, 1973.

Lyons, Diane. "Witchcraft, Gender, Power and Intimate Relations in Mura Compounds in Déla, Northern Cameroon." *World Archeology* 29, no. 3 (1998): 344–62.

MacGaffey, Wyatt. "Complexity, Astonishment, and Power: the Visual Vocabulary of Kongo Minkisi." *Journal of Southern African Studies* 14, no. 2 (1988): 188–203.

MacGaffey, Wyatt. *Kongo Political Culture: The Conceptual Challenge of the Particular.* Bloomington: Indiana University Press, 2000.

MacGaffey, Wyatt. "The Personhood of Ritual Objects: Kongo 'Minkisi'." *Ethnofoor,* Jaarg 3.1(1990): 45–61.

MacGaffey, Wyatt. *Religion and Society in Central Africa: The BaKongo of Lower Zaire.* Chicago: University of Chicago Press, 1986.

Marshall, Lorna J. *Nyae Nyae !Kung Beliefs and Rites.* Cambridge, MA: Peabody Museum of Archaeology and Ethnology, Harvard University, 1999.

Matory, J. Lorand. *Black Atlantic Religion: Tradition, Transnationalism, and Matriarchy in the Afro-Brazilian Candomblé.* Princeton, NJ: Princeton University Press, 2005.

McAllister, Patrick A. *Xhosa Beer Drinking Rituals: Power, Practice and Performance in the South African Rural Periphery.* Durham, NC: Carolina Academic Press, 2006.

Metuh, Emefie Ikenga. *Comparative Studies of African Traditional Religions.* Onitsha, Nigeria: IMICO Publishers, 1987.

Muller, Carl Ann. *Rituals of Fertility and the Sacrifice of Desire: Nazarite Women's Performance in South Africa.* Chicago: University of Chicago Press, 1999.

Mwaura, Philomena Njeri. "The Role of Charismatic Christianity in Reshaping the Religious Scene in Africa: The Case of Kenya." In *Christianity in Africa and the African Diaspora: The Appropriation of a Scattered Heritage,* edited by Afe Adogame, Roswith Gerloff, and Klaus Hock, 180–92. London: Continuum, 2008.

"Mythology of Black Africa." *New Larousse Encyclopedia of Mythology.* New Edition. London: Hamlyn Publishing Group, 1968.

Niehaus, Isak A. "Witch-hunting & Political Legitimacy: Continuity and Change in Green Valley, Lebowa." *Africa* 63, no. 4 (1993): 498–530.

Northcott, Cecil. *Robert Moffat: Pioneer in Africa 1817–1870.* London: Lutterworth, 1961.

Nunley, John W. "West African Sculpture: Sacred Space, Spirit, and Power." *Bulletin (St. Louis Art Museum)* New Series 16, no. 4 (1983): 1–41.

Ocholla-Ayayo, A. B. C. *Traditional Ideology and Ethics among the Southern Luo.* Uppsala: [Stockholm: Scandinavian Institute of African Studies; Almquist & Wiksell international, distr.], 1976.

Further reading

Olupona, Jacob K. "African Indigenous Religions." In *Introduction to World Religions: Communities and Cultures*, edited by Jacob Neusner, 291–308. Nashville: Abingdon Press, 2010.

Olupona, Jacob K. "African Religion." *Global Religions: An Introduction*, edited by Mark Juergensmeyer, 78–86. Oxford: Oxford University Press, 2003.

Olupona, Jacob K. "African Traditional Religions." *Worldmark Encyclopedia of Religious Practices*. Vol.1, *Religions and Denominations*, edited by Thomas Riggs, 1–21. Detroit: Thomas Gale, 2006.

Olupona, Jacob K. "Owner of the Day and Regulator of the Universe: Ifa Divination and Healing among the Yoruba of Southwestern Nigeria." In Winkelman and Peek, *Divination and Healing*, 103–17. Tucson: University of Arizona Press, 2004.

Olupona, Jacob K. "Sacred Cosmos: An Ethnography of African Indigenous Religious Traditions." In *African Americans and the Bible: Sacred Texts and Social Textures*, edited by Vincent L. Wimbush, 163–78. New York: Continuum, 2000.

Olupona, Jacob K. "To Praise and to Reprimand: Ancestors and Spirituality in African Society and Culture." In *Ancestors in Post-Contact Religion: Roots, Ruptures, and Modernity's Memory*, edited by Steven J. Friesen, 49–66. Cambridge, MA: Distributed by Harvard University Press for the Center for the Study of World Religions Harvard Divinity School, 2001.

Olupona, Jacob K. "Yoruba Goddesses and Sovereignty in Southwestern Nigeria." In *Goddesses Who Rule*, edited by Elisabeth Benard and Beverly Moon, 119–32. Oxford: Oxford University Press, 2000.

Olupona, Jacob K., with Sola Ajibade. "Ekun Iyawo: Bridal Tears in Marriage Rites of Passage among the Oyo-Yoruba of Nigeria." In *Holy Tears: Weeping in the Religious Imagination*, edited by Kimberley Christine Patton and John Stratton Hawley, 165–77. Princeton, NJ: Princeton University Press, 2005.

Parfitt, Tudor. *Journey to the Vanished City: The Search for the Lost Tribe of Israel*. London: Phoenix, 1992, 1997.

Parrinder, Geoffrey. *African Mythology*. London: Hamlyn, 1967.

Peek, Laura. "'Prosperity Is the Promise of God'." *Times Online* (England), March 16, 2003.

Peek, Philip M., ed. *African Divination Systems: Ways of Knowing*. Bloomington: Indiana University Press, 1991.

Peek, Philip M. "The Power of Words in African Verbal Arts." *Journal of American Folklore* 94, no. 371 (1981): 19–43.

Pemberton, John, III, and Funso S. Afolayan. *Yoruba Sacred Kingship: "A Power Like That of the Gods."* Washington, DC: Smithsonian Institution Press, 1996.

Perrois, Louis. *Fang.* Visions of Africa Series 2. Milan: 5 Continents, 2006.

Phillips, Ruth B. *Representing Woman: Sande Masquerades of the Mende of Sierra Leone.* Los Angeles: UCLA Fowler Museum of Cultural History, 1995.

Platvoet, Jan, James Cox, and Jacob K. Olupọna, eds. *The Study of Religions in Africa: Past, Present and Prospects.* Cambridge, UK: Roots and Branches, 1996.

"Preacher to Hang for Sin Burnings," *British Broadcasting Corporation Online,* January 11, 2007.

Ray, Benjamin C. *African Religions: Symbol, Ritual, and Community.* 2nd ed. Upper Saddle River, NJ: Prentice Hall, 2000.

Reynolds, Barrie. *Magic, Divination and Witchcraft among the Barotse of Northern Rhodesia.* Berkeley: University of California Press, 1963.

Roberts, Mary Nooter. *Luba.* Milan, Italy: 5 Continents Editions, 2007.

Roberts, Mary Nooter. "Memory: Luba Art and the Making of History." *African Arts* 29, no. 1 (1996): 22–35; 101–3.

Roscoe, John. *The Baganda: An Account of Their Native Customs and Beliefs.* London: Macmillan, 1911.

Ross, Mabel H., and Barbara K. Walker. *"On Another Day . . .": Tales Told Among the Nkundo of Zäire.* Hamden, CT: Archon, 1979.

Sanders, Todd. *Beyond Bodies: Rainmaking and Sense Making in Tanzania.* Anthropological Horizons Series 32. Toronto: University of Toronto Press, 2008.

Setiloane, Gabriel M. *The Image of God among the Sotho-Tswana.* Rotterdam: Balkema, 1976.

Shaw, Rosalind. "Splitting Truths from Darkness: Espitemological Aspects of Temne Divination." In *African Divination Systems: Ways of Knowing,* edited by Philip M. Peek, 137–51. Bloomington: Indiana University Press, 1991.

Sieber, Roy, and Roslyn Adele Walker. *African Art in the Cycle of Life.* Washington, DC: Smithsonian Institution Press, 1988.

Simonse, Simon. *Kings of Disaster: Dualism, Centralism and the Scapegoat King in Southeastern Sudan.* Leiden: E. J. Brill, 1992.

Somé, Malidoma Patrice. *The Healing Wisdom of Africa: Finding Life Purpose through Nature, Ritual, and Community.* London: Thorsons, 1999.

Steegstra, Marijke. *Resilient Rituals: Krobo Initiation and the Politics of Culture in Ghana*. Modernity and Belonging Series. Münster: Lit, 2004.

Steiger-Hayley, T. T. *The Anatomy of Lango Religion and Groups*. Cambridge: Cambridge University Press, 1947.

Stroeken, Koen. "In Search of the Real: The Healing Contingency of Sukuma Divination." In *Divination and Healing: Potent Vision* , edited by Michael Winkelman and Philip M. Peek, 29–54. Tucson: University of Arizona Press, 2004.

Stroeken, Koen. "Stalking the Stalker: A Chwezi Initiation into Spirit Possession and Experiential Structure." *Journal of the Royal Anthropological Institute (N.S.)* 12 (2006): 785–802.

Sussman, Robert W., and Linda K. Sussman. "Divination among the Sakalava of Madagascar." In *Extrasensory Ecology: Parapsychology and Anthropology*, edited by Joseph K. Long, 271–91. Metuchen, NJ: Scarecrow Press, 1977.

Tcherkezoff, Serge. *Dual Classification Reconsidered: Nyamwezi Sacred Kingship and Other Examples*. Translated by Maritn Thom. Cambridge: Cambridge University Press, 1987.

Thompson, Robert Farris. "Face of the Gods: the Artists and Their Altars." *African Arts* 28, no. 1 (1995): 50–61.

Tiesh, Luisah. *Jambalaya: The Natural Woman's Book of Personal Charms and Practical Rituals*. San Francisco: Harper & Row, 1985.

Turner, Victor W. *The Lozi People of North-Western Rhodesia*. London: International African Institute, 1952.

Van Binsbergen, Wim. "Regional and Historical Connections of Four-Tablet Divination in Southern Africa." *Journal of Religion in Africa* 25, no. 1 (1996): 2–29.

Van Wyk, Gary. "Illuminated Signs. Style and Meaning in the Beadwork of the Xhosa- and Zulu Speaking Peoples." *African Arts* 36, no. 3 (2003): 12–33, 93–94.

Vérin, Pierre, and Naricelo Rajaonarimanana. "Divination in Madagascar: The Antemoro Case and the Diffusion of Divination." In Peek, *African Divination Systems*, 53–68.

Visonà, Monica Blackmun, Robin Poynor, and Herbert M. Cole. *History of Art in Africa*. New York: Abrams, 2001.

Ward, Martha. *Voodoo Queen: The Spirited Lives of Marie Laveau*. Jackson: University Press of Mississippi, 2004.

Whyte, Susan Reynolds. "Knowledge and Power in Nyole Divination." In Peek, *African Divination Systems*, 153–71.

Wilentz, Amy. "Voodoo in Haiti Today." *Grand Street* 6, no. 2 (1987): 105–23.

"Witchcraft and sorcery, African." In *Wordsworth Dictionary of Beliefs and Religions*. edited by Rosemary Goring, 564–65. Herefordshire: Wordsworth Reference, 1992.

Zuesse, Evan M. *Ritual Cosmos: the Sanctification of Life in African Religions*. Athens: Ohio University Press, 1979.

Index

A

Index

ONLINE CATALOGUE
A Very Short Introduction

Our online catalogue is designed to make it easy to find your ideal Very Short Introduction. View the entire collection by subject area, watch author videos, read sample chapters, and download reading guides.

http://fds.oup.com/www.oup.co.uk/general/vsi/index.html

SOCIAL MEDIA
Very Short Introduction

Join our community
www.oup.com/vsi

- Join us online at the official Very Short Introductions **Facebook** page.
- Access the thoughts and musings of our authors with our online **blog**.
- Sign up for our monthly **e-newsletter** to receive information on all new titles publishing that month.
- Browse the full range of Very Short Introductions online.
- Read **extracts** from the Introductions for free.
- Visit our library of **Reading Guides**. These guides, written by our expert authors will help you to question again, why you think what you think.
- If you are a teacher or lecturer you can order inspection copies quickly and simply via our website.